BM

The Student's Guide to Peer Mentoring

For a complete listing of all our titles in this area please visit
www.palgravehighered.com/study-skills

Palgrave Study Skills

Business Degree Success
Career Skills
Cite Them Right (10th edn)
Critical Thinking Skills (3rd edn)
Dissertations and Project Reports
e-Learning Skills (2nd edn)
The Exam Skills Handbook (2nd edn)
Get Sorted
The Graduate Career Guidebook
Great Ways to Learn Anatomy and Physiology
  (2nd edn)
How to Begin Studying English Literature (4th edn)
How to Study Foreign Languages
How to Study Linguistics (2nd edn)
How to Use Your Reading in Your Essays (2nd edn)
How to Write Better Essays (3rd edn)
How to Write Your Undergraduate Dissertation
  (2nd edn)
Improve Your Grammar (2nd edn)
Information Skills
The International Student Handbook
The Mature Student's Guide to Writing (3rd edn)
The Mature Student's Handbook
The Palgrave Student Planner
The Personal Tutor's Handbook
Practical Criticism
Presentation Skills for Students (3rd edn)
The Principles of Writing in Psychology
Professional Writing (3rd edn)
Researching Online
Skills for Success (3rd edn)
Smart Thinking
The Student's Guide to Writing (3rd edn)
The Student Phrase Book
Study Skills Connected
Study Skills for International Postgraduates
Study Skills for Speakers of English as a Second
  Language
The Study Skills Handbook (4th edn)
Studying History (3rd edn)

Studying Law (4th edn)
Studying Modern Drama (2nd edn)
Studying Psychology (2nd edn)
Success in Academic Writing
Teaching Study Skills and Supporting Learning
The Undergraduate Research Handbook
The Work-Based Learning Student Handbook
  (2nd edn)
Work Placements – A Survival Guide for Students
Write it Right (2nd edn)
Writing for Engineers (3rd edn)
Writing for Law
Writing for Nursing and Midwifery Students
  (2nd edn)
Writing History Essays (2nd edn)
You2Uni: Decide. Prepare. Apply

Pocket Study Skills

14 Days to Exam Success
Analyzing a Case Study
Brilliant Writing Tips for Students
Completing Your PhD
Doing Research
Getting Critical (2nd edn)
Planning Your Dissertation
Planning Your Essay (2nd edn)
Planning Your PhD
Posters and Presentations
Reading and Making Notes (2nd edn)
Referencing and Understanding Plagiarism
Reflective Writing
Report Writing
Science Study Skills
Studying with Dyslexia
Success in Groupwork
Time Management
Where's Your Argument?
Writing for University (2nd edn)

Palgrave Career Skills

Excel at Graduate Interviews

The Student's Guide to Peer Mentoring

Get More From Your University Experience

Louise Frith, Gina May and Amanda Pocklington

 macmillan education   palgrave

First published 2017 by
PALGRAVE

Palgrave in the UK is an imprint of Macmillan Publishers Limited, registered in England, company number 785998, of 4 Crinan Street, London, N1 9XW.

Palgrave® and Macmillan® are registered trademarks in the United States, the United Kingdom, Europe and other countries.

ISBN 978–1–137–59995–7 paperback

This book is printed on paper suitable for recycling and made from fully managed and sustained forest sources. Logging, pulping and manufacturing processes are expected to conform to the environmental regulations of the country of origin.

A catalogue record for this book is available from the British Library.

A catalog record for this book is available from the Library of Congress.

Contents

Acknowledgements

Our special thanks go to colleagues at the University of Kent in the Student Learning Advisory Service and at the University of Exeter in the Academic Skills and Engagement Team. We would also like to thank all of the students who have worked as peer mentors and volunteered as mentees over the years at both Kent and Exeter Universities. We have benefited from their commitment, enthusiasm and feedback on peer mentoring. In particular we would like to acknowledge the support we have received from Palgrave editorial and production teams and in particular the help we have been given by Commissioning Editor Helen Caunce.

Introduction

As you start to read this book, try to think about the people throughout your education who have been influential. They might have been a classroom assistant or a teacher during your early years as a child at school; a sports or music teacher who inspired you; or possibly a friend or older family member who supported your development or encouraged you to persist when you felt like giving up. The role other people play in your educational journey can have a huge impact on your development, so the role of peer mentor is of great importance. This book is aimed primarily at peer mentors in higher education settings. It will provide you with a context, and framework for mentoring and give you specific guidance on some of the common issues and tricky aspects of being a mentor so that you get the most out of the experience and your mentees find your input helpful.

We know that peer-led learning is a growing and vital area in higher education that has the potential to transform the way in which learning takes place. We also hope that academic skills practitioners and others who support the development of mentoring activities in universities will find this a useful handbook to refer to. Although there is a logical progression through each of the chapters, it is not necessary to read this book from cover to cover. Each chapter has exercises within it to enable you to pause and think about your response to what you have read. These exercises can be done individually, but they also lend themselves to group work, so the book can be used in training or other mentor support programmes. Hopefully it is something you will dip in and out of during your time as a mentor, and it may also be useful to you after you finish mentoring as an aide-memoire for the experiences you had as a mentor. It may also help you to reflect on and communicate the skills you have developed to others, such as employers or admissions tutors. Although this book can be used to support mentor training, it is not a training manual and it certainly should not be used instead of targeted mentor training. It is a student guide to mentoring, which we hope will enhance your understanding of the role mentors play and help you to reflect on your experience of mentoring.

What is peer-led learning?

Peer-led learning, also referred to in this book as peer mentoring, has been around since the 1990s in the UK higher education sector. It is known by a wide variety of terms. The most common of these are peer-assisted learning (PAL) and peer-assisted study sessions (PASS), but there are many other terms that are used to describe the study and academic support that students give to students. This type of mentoring derives from supplemental instruction, which was developed in the in the 1970s at the University of Missouri Kansas City. Peer-led learning is now a common feature in many UK universities and is also becoming widespread in other European and Pacific universities. The concept of mentoring draws on educational research from a number of different perspectives, which emphasises, first, the importance of students feeling connected at a personal level to their university; second, collaborative learning pedagogy, which fosters links and interconnections between students to improve their learning; and, finally, mentor support for students to embrace their new academic identity.

Why is peer-led learning growing in popularity?

Peer-led learning is gaining momentum, nationally and internationally. It is now found in nearly all UK universities and across a broad range of disciplines. Peer-led learning schemes are often attached to specific modules which students find difficult, the emphasis being on support for difficult modules rather than targeting weak students. Mentoring can also be focused on social support functions. These types of mentoring scheme are often termed buddying. Many peer-led learning schemes are targeted at specific groups of students, such as international students, BME students, mature or part-time students, and students on placement, and there is also a growing practice of online mentoring. In addition to these targeted forms of mentoring there are an increasing number of universities that are able to offer mentor-development opportunities to work as a mentor for more than a year. This gives experienced mentors the chance to support incoming mentors and get involved in their training. The context of higher education has changed dramatically; during the past 20 years the numbers of students entering university has increased significantly. University can be a daunting experience for some new students because programmes of study can be very large, meaning that they may not necessarily have a personal relationship with their lecturers, especially in core first-year modules. Mentors play an important role in bridging the gap between new students and academic staff. Therefore an essential element of peer-led learning is that students make a personal connection and feel supported to study and persist at university.

What are the benefits of mentoring?

If you are considering mentoring you should know that there is a lot you can get out of the experience. It is now widely accepted that all stakeholders in the mentoring relationship benefit from building active partnerships between staff and students, institutions and students, and among students themselves. Mentors are sometimes described as the 'real winners' in mentoring schemes. This is because the evidence suggests that you get significant benefit from working in a mentoring role (Keenan, 2014). For example, it increases your confidence in both an academic and a social context; you consolidate your learning by revising course materials and explaining study techniques and it gives you opportunities to improve your interpersonal skills. All of this results in mentors generally doing better in their studies and going on to graduate employment afterwards (Kent, Student Success Conference 2016). For mentees there are also significant benefits: they have an opportunity to learn in small groups in a supportive environment with peers. The focus of PAL groups is discussion, so mentees have a chance to ask questions and air views, which can then help them to participate more confidently in seminars and lectures. There are also significant social benefits for mentees because, through their mentor, they can make connections with others on their course. This is often a crucial factor in new students' sense of belonging and persistence at university. Academic staff are generally supportive of mentoring schemes. The benefit for them is that some of the administrative questions that would have been directed at them are fielded by mentors. In addition to this, mentors can reinforce good study messages to new students about attendance, time management and keeping up with reading. Finally, from the point of view of the institution, the benefits are clear: mentors embody values which universities are eager to promote, such as caring for students, student-centred learning and inter-cultural communication.

Who are peer mentors?

There is no *ideal type* for mentoring, but, as you will read in Chapter 4, there are common characteristics and values which mentors tend to have. Mentors are generally motivated by a wish to help other students and put something back into their university experience. Anyone can become a mentor; you do not need to be a first-class student or to have had any particular experiences of university study. In fact, it is quite often the case that students who have overcome difficult experiences during their studies make great mentors because they have developed resilience and worked out strategies to succeed at university that they can pass on. A basic requirement is an enjoyment of study and a wish to pass that on to others. Mentors often have an eye on their own employability profile and are motivated to become a mentor because they can see that it is an opportunity for them to develop and demonstrate skills that are hard to acquire in other contexts. This often attracts students who may be interested in a future role that involves teaching, training, managing or coaching.

What skills do you need to have?

As a mentor you will develop in the role, but there are some skills you should either already have or have an interest in acquiring. Good communication skills are really a cornerstone in any successful mentoring relationship. It is not easy to support others while also studying yourself, so some of what you learn as a mentor is how to prioritise your own work, and how to set and maintain clear boundaries. As well as this, you need to be organised, and to work well both individually and in a team. These skills are highly prized by employers so it is important that as a mentor you record the work that you do so that you are able to give concrete examples to show that you have these skills. Chapters 8 and 9 give you lots of direction relating to this, and you may also find that your university students' union or careers advice service will be able to give you further support in identifying your skills before and after mentoring.

Chapter summaries

The book is divided into three sections. The first section explains mentors' roles, motivations and characteristics. Chapter 2 gives a detailed explanation of the roles that peer mentors play in universities and how they fit into university structures. It explains different common models of peer mentoring and asks you to think about the model in your own university. There is discussion of the cross-cultural role that mentors can play and information on the limitations of peer-led learning. Chapter 3 presents research into what motivates students to become mentors. It includes case studies from a variety of students about why they wanted to become a peer mentor and encourages you to reflect on your reasons for becoming a mentor. Chapter 4 draws on Terrion and Leonard's (2007) typology of ten characteristics for successful peer mentors. It also includes a self-evaluation questionnaire so that you can evaluate your own characteristics and assess your suitability for mentoring.

In the middle section, Chapters 5 and 6 provide detailed examples of the types of academic and social support that peer mentors provide. Chapter 5 gives an introduction to academic support skills for mentoring, such as learning styles, small group teaching, participation and feedback. It includes case studies and examples from different subjects. This provides some contrasts between mentoring practice in the disciplines. It gives advice on how to deliver support and when to draw the line between support and dependency. Chapter 6 looks in more detail at the types of social support situations that peer mentors may encounter. It gives an introduction to communication skills such as active listening, confidentiality and reflective practice. It includes case studies and advice on how to offer support while maintaining boundaries to protect both the mentor and the mentee.

The last section of the book examines some of the difficulties that mentors may encounter, as well as identifying the academic and employability skills you derive from mentoring and how you can articulate these to others. In Chapter 7 the power relationships between mentors and mentees, and between mentors and the university, are considered. It looks at different models of power and voice, and puts mentoring into the context of contemporary higher education that emphasises student satisfaction. The chapter provides a series of difficult scenarios which mentors may face within their role. It considers particularly the issue of mentees not engaging with mentoring and what solutions there are for this, with the focus on online mentoring. There are suggestions as to how a mentor can deal with these types of situation and where to seek further sources of support. Chapter 8 looks at the academic confidence and enhanced study skills that students gain from being a mentor. It also considers the employability skills that mentors gain from their experience, giving short statements from alumni and students who have been mentored on placement or in voluntary work about the value of mentoring, and how the skills they gained as a mentor have helped them in their life after university. Chapter 9 uses reflective practice models to enable you to reflect on your experience of being a mentor and to start to articulate it. It features questions to help you write about your experience. The last section of the book, comprising Chapter 10, draws some conclusions.

We hope that you will find the book a useful companion during your time as a peer mentor. Although, at first, mentoring might seem overwhelming because you might have high expectations of what you want to achieve, as time progresses and you get to know your mentees and the role you play in their development, we hope you will find that it is a useful and enjoyable experience. Previous mentors have described their experience of mentoring as 'intense and very rewarding'. We hope that you will derive similar emotions from your mentoring experience, which will develop your confidence and enhance your skills.

The Role of Peer Mentoring in Universities

2

By the end of this chapter you will:

- have an overview of the position of peer mentoring in universities
- have an understanding of the role, responsibilities and boundaries of being a peer mentor
- have an understanding of the connections between peer mentoring and other university services
- have an appreciation of the different models and delivery formats
- have a range of case studies exemplifying different models to compare to your own experience.

Mentoring in some form has existed for as long as human beings have interacted with each other. It is common knowledge that parents guide their children, who in turn support their friends, but employers, teachers and coaches, to name but a few, also offer support to others. You have no doubt provided informal mentoring to friends without classifying it as such; it is just part of a normal friendship. Peer mentoring programmes in universities are more structured than a friendship relationship. They generally have goals and objectives which might pertain to similar benefits as friendship but they are not intended as replacements for normal friendship support. Generally, as a peer mentor you tread a fine line between being a friend/confidante and a tutor, taking on neither role in its full form but assuming some aspects of each. Understanding the intricacies of the role of peer mentor and the role of peer mentoring in higher education will take time and effort to master.

Peer mentoring in higher education has been expanding for a number of years. The number of peer programmes in existence worldwide has not been formally identified but their existence is certainly evident in all countries that have a formal education system. This can be seen from a review of university websites and other online media. Another indication is the growing number of texts and papers published worldwide in the field of peer mentoring and its associated areas. The breadth and depth of the types of peer support programme have unsurprisingly followed a similar expansion path. There are various reasons for this. Many institutions view peer programmes as part of the menu of strategies to address the wider issues they face, including widening participation, retention, achievement, graduate destinations, student wellbeing and the student experience (Ody and

Carey, 2013). In light of this range of purposes you may not be surprised to find that the location of peer mentoring within university structures varies greatly across institutions, from large central programmes to small student-led groups. Similarly, the role of the peer mentor also varies across departments, institutions and countries. The one thing tying them all together is that the role of the peer mentor is to help and support their fellow students.

This chapter will look at various aspects of the role in its difference contexts, along with the connections with other services and will help you understand what peer mentoring is at your university.

Activity 2.1

Relating to your own experience

It might be helpful for you to cast your mind back to when you first thought of going to university.

- How did you feel?
- What concerns did you have?
- What expectations did you have?

Then think about after you arrived.

- How did you deal with the transition to university and the journey through the first year?
- Consider who you felt helped you with this process: was it a support service at the university, a tutor, another student or a mixture of these?

Generally it is a mixture of these avenues that students seek and receive support and guidance from. So what does a peer mentor offer that others might not?

What is peer mentoring at university for?

Universities have a multifaceted role within the society within which they are established. First and foremost they are centres for learning, but they are also much more than this. Education provides a backbone for the development of a society, supporting areas such as inclusion, knowledge, freedom of speech, research, debate, inquiry and open-mindedness. To aid in these far-reaching ideals, universities employ an extensive range of strategies: peer mentoring is one such strategy offering an avenue to work towards achieving these overarching goals. Peer mentoring is generally seen as a complementary form of support for students that might address academic, transitional or pastoral objectives as fits the arena in which the programme sits. For example, a strategic peer mentoring goal may be raising student achievement and have an academic-based objective relating to the societal goal of increasing knowledge. Therefore as a peer mentor your role is pivotal in not only the aims of the programme but also the goals of the university and the development of society.

In order to meet these varying objectives effectively, peer programmes have to be structured in different ways. To this end, many institutions have adopted different models and terms for both the programmes and the roles involved. When you review texts on peer mentoring, one of the first things to understand is what is meant by peer mentoring at university. Unfortunately this is not an easy task, partly due to a lack of consensus concerning the terms used for mentoring programmes. In a review of literature about peer-assisted learning (PAL), Green (2011) recognised this somewhat bewildering array of terminology in existence in the research and reports reviewed. You may find perhaps only one or indeed several different terms in use at your institution. Examples of the terms used might include peer-assisted study sessions (PASS), PAL, peer mentoring and peer buddying, to name some of the more common titles. There is perhaps some more specific meaning attached to these which connects with the goals of the programme, which is addressed later in this chapter. However, there are some common aspects of the majority of peer programmes which we can use as a basis for our discussion of the role of the peer mentor and peer mentoring programmes at university.

Generally, as a peer mentor you will be of a similar standing to your mentees. That is to say, peer mentors are perhaps in a year above their mentees but have no particular authority or control over their mentees, unlike the situation often found in employment. Hence, ideally, as a university peer mentor you are a role model for your mentees to emulate. You support this through advice and guidance based on your own university experiences and your knowledge of the peer programme goals. Hence it is important for you to understand your peer programme structure and goals, as well as your specific role within that framework.

There is no universal, meaningful definition provided for the term 'peer mentor'. A quick review of texts, papers and university websites reveals a wide variety of descriptions of the peer mentor role. There are also role descriptors for peer leaders, peer leader supervisors, peer tutors and peer assistants, to list but a few of the terms used for such positions.

Activity 2.2

Role descriptors

Look at the example role descriptors for mentors provided here and compare them with the role descriptors provided at your own institution. Discuss the appropriateness of these with your fellow peer mentors or mentees. What do you feel the role should encompass, and what should the goals be?

Mentors:

- facilitate group discussion and exercises around the weekly material
- provide a sounding board for ideas

- promote understanding by re-examining course material as a group
- liaise regularly with relevant academics to maintain correct pace
- feed back general information to the school
- provide support and encouragement
- promote independent learning
- establish a climate of trust and support.

Mentees:

- engage with their mentor regularly
- respond to emails and other contact
- inform their mentor if they want to end the support or if they are absent
- be aware that mentors are there for support but not to do work for mentees.

Academic school:

- identify suitable mentors
- allocate rooms
- provide equipment (pens, flipchart paper, etc.)
- facilitate liaison between mentors and academic staff (liaison tutor) regarding course/module content, subject-specific information, collection of feedback on mentees' general understanding.

Central learning support team:

- train student mentors
- supervise mentors (visit sessions, review meetings)
- advise mentors (pedagogy, activities, group management)
- provide an objective outside view ('a sounding-board' for ideas/troubles)
- provide external support in case of disputes
- officially acknowledge mentors' contribution.

The place of peer mentoring in universities

Some peer programmes are situated within a central university team and are funded, organised and managed centrally. At other universities it is the students' union that runs a central peer programme. Conversely, in other universities, peer programmes are operated within a single module by a single tutor or set up by motivated students. Perhaps you are one of these motivated students. These examples might be viewed as being at opposite ends of the organisational continuum, with other peer programmes found somewhere along this structural line. Obviously, funding and resources are key factors in deciding where peer support is situated, which is somewhat dictated by the university's aims and objectives.

Activity 2.3

Institutional aims and objectives

Are you aware of your university's aims and objectives and how these might impact on support for peer programmes? If you are planning on setting up a peer programme, this is likely to be useful information to gather.

There is an ever-growing number of institutions which operate a centrally managed university-wide programme. These are often focused on new entrant transition providing pastoral support to students, easing the process of adapting to life at university. These students are often living away from home for the first time and some have the additional stress of relocating to a new country. You may well be familiar with the common terms in use here such as 'buddying', 'peer mentoring', 'student ambassadors' and 'parenting', with the providers of that support named 'buddies', 'mentors', 'ambassadors' or 'parents'. Smaller-scale programmes are often developed by enthusiastic staff members who have recognised the benefits of peer support for their students and developed a peer programme within their department or module. These are often in response to the recognition of a difficult aspect of a course where students tend to struggle and would benefit from some extra support, so the support is for difficult areas of the curriculum rather than for struggling students. Similarly, there are a number of situations where students have experienced challenges within a course or identified a need for alternative support and have responded by creating their own peer programme. You may well be one of these students or perhaps you are considering setting up a programme. This text aims to provide guidance and information for peer leaders/mentors and so will also aid you in the development of a new programme should you decide to do that. However, these peer programmes should not be confused with students' union societies, which are also set up and run by students to pursue a common interest. Such societies might be related to any topic, from philosophy to playing frisbee and are open to any student at the institution, whereas peer programmes tend to be centred on a particular cohort of students. Some of these societies are discipline-oriented and often add a distinct subject support avenue for students. Hence it might be advantageous to ascertain if there is a society aligned to your peer programme area and make appropriate connections with this group to ensure that they work as complementary support avenues for students. Hopefully it is now apparent that there is not a one-size-fits-all situation when it comes to peer mentoring. This is partly why there is a confusion of terms in use, not only across institutions but within them too.

Activity 2.4

Peer programmes at your institution

Do you know how many peer programmes exist at your institution?
What types of peer programme exist?
Is there more than one type?
What terms are currently used to refer to peer support programmes and their stakeholders at your institution?

Models of peer mentoring

As you can see, the particular focus of a peer programme tends to be directed by the specific goals of the programme organisers and has led to the adoption of a variety of models and terms for both programmes and those involved in them. Much has been written on the subject, recognising this worldwide diversity of practice and terminology (Ody and Carey, 2013).

Many peer programmes involve a cross-year model where a limited number of higher-year students support a group of lower-year students (often referred to as a vertical model). There are also examples of in-year peer mentoring (often referred to as a horizontal model) where same-year mentors might be selected by tutors or voted in by the student group themselves. The more unusual setup (reverse vertical model) is where lower-year students support upper-year students. Such a situation might be seen where a course tends to attract mature students who might benefit from specific support in a particular area where lower-year students are more experienced, such as technical IT developments. The above terms of 'vertical and horizontal models' describe the year of study of peer mentors to mentees. However, these are not the only model descriptors used for peer mentoring.

Mentoring programmes differ in terms of structure and organisation, which might be seen as classifying them into other model types. The university or college-wide transition support model often involves a relatively ad hoc meeting approach whereby mentors are assigned a small number of first year students who can request support as and when needed. This format can have a number of titles, including 'peer support', 'peer mentoring', 'parenting' and, 'transition buddies'. A slightly more structured model is where a pair of peer mentors are assigned a small group of lower-year students and they set up relatively regular informal group meetings. Here the mentees can discuss issues related to their student experience or perhaps general aspects of study. Such a model might be referred to as a peer mentoring or perhaps a PAL programme. The most structured approach tends to be centred on a module or subject area. Meetings are timetabled and leaders facilitate discussion, addressing module or subject topics. This type of model is often referred to as PAL, or as 'peer tutoring' or a 'peer-assisted study session' (PASS) programme. A common aspect of all peer programmes is the opportunity provided to mentors to ask questions and gain support from the programme organiser through debrief meetings.

Peer programme model types and descriptors

Style	Common titles	Common general aspects
1. Structured	PASS, PAL, peer tutoring	Regular weekly meetings, timetabled/scheduled, structured, academic subject based, group sessions, regular mentor debriefs, meetings generally one or two mentors to several mentees per group
2. Semi-structured	Peer coaching, PAL, peer mentoring	Regular meetings, scheduled, possibly timetabled, at least semi-structured, subject related based, group sessions, at least semi-regular mentor debriefs, meetings generally one or two mentors to several mentees per group
3. Un-structured	Buddying, parenting, peer support, mentoring	Ad hoc meetings, pastoral and transition support, not timetabled, participant request oriented, occasional mentor debriefs, meetings generally one or two mentors to one or two mentees, transition and pastoral based

As the table of peer programme model types indicates, these varying peer programme structures tend to utilise slightly different session structures. The PASS is generally somewhat more dictated by the module and its programme of lectures, whereas the ad hoc unstructured programmes are completely directed by the concerns of the mentees. These structural differences result in the PASS being more geared towards identifying areas of challenge posed by a module's content and trying to assist the mentees in gaining an understanding of these aspects. This is commonly achieved through facilitated discussion and guidance as mentees try example worksheets and problems around specific module topics. The semi-structured (e.g. PAL, peer coaching) style sessions more generally address the overall topics of the discipline and/or the associated study skills needed to successfully complete the course. Again, this involves facilitated discussion of general subject areas or may look at pertinent study skills areas to assist mentees in developing these important skill sets. The unstructured ad hoc (e.g. buddying, peer support) style sessions are arranged between mentors and mentees, generally at the mentees' request. These are more meeting-style sessions where mentees can raise concerns or ask questions, which mentors either answer or signpost mentees to other support services.

Example of structured (PASS) session plan:

- Welcome, introductions and ice breaker – as appropriate
- Briefly summarise previous PASS session – as appropriate
- Invite recap of previous lecture(s) by mentees – with prompts as needed
- Identify areas of concern/challenge through individual, pair and group activities
- Mentees discuss these areas – mentors facilitate
- Consider worksheet, seminar topic or reading set by module lead/tutor – as appropriate
- Mentors identify areas of common concern to feed back to module lead/tutor at debrief meeting
- Mentors makes notes of areas addressed and close session

Example of semi-structured (e.g. PAL) session plan:

- Welcome, introductions and ice breaker – as appropriate
- Briefly summarise previous session – as appropriate
- Invite suggestions for session topic by mentees, or topic given by mentor
- Mentees discuss topic areas or consider study skills aspect – mentors facilitate
- Mentors identify areas of common knowledge/skill gap or lack of understanding to feed back to module lead/tutor at debrief meeting
- Mentors makes notes of areas addressed and close session

Example of unstructured (e.g. buddy scheme) session plan:

- Introductions and general ice breaker discussion – as appropriate
- Check any actions taken as a result of previous meeting – as appropriate
- Invite mentee to raise concerns
- Discuss issues and possible avenues to address these (signposting as appropriate)
- Note actions suggested for mentee and any follow-up activities for mentor, including possible next meeting date – as appropriate
- Close meeting

There are of course other peer-supported activities, such as peer assessment, peer projects and peer tutor groups, but these tend to be part of the main curriculum. Such activities are generally organised by a module tutor and conducted in a classroom setting solely under the control and management of the tutor. These types of peer-related task are outside the remit of this text but it can be helpful to realise that they may well occur at your institution. They do tend to add another layer of confusion about the terms used as they tend to adopt similar titles for the parties involved.

Examples of peer programme models

The following examples of peer programmes are described to help you understand the different models and types of peer programme. You may find that there are similar programmes and models at your university or you may find that your institution adopts a different approach.

Example 1: PASS scheme in a maths module within a business school

Maths is often considered a challenging topic of study. Gaining an understanding of one aspect can be dependent on having clear comprehension of and skill relating to another. Students can feel stuck and not able to progress in the module due to a lack of understanding of a specific part. PASS have proved popular in maths modules due to the opportunity to embed such skills and understanding. It can be that a different approach to explanation is all it takes for the penny to drop and the maths process becomes clear. By providing weekly example problem worksheets, mentors can help mentees pinpoint where they have difficulties, and by using careful questioning techniques they can work through these sheets. Mentees appreciate the regularity of peer study sessions as it means that all students can keep up with the module. Mentors note they also benefit from recapping previously studied areas, helping them to embed their learning too. Mentors are also supported through regular debrief sessions with the programme organiser and module lead.

Example 2: PAL programme in geography

Many disciplines have specific approaches to study. Geography uses field trips to highlight aspects of the course in more practical and visual terms. These field trips are really appreciated by students as they become aware of the benefits to learning that these activities offer. However, they can be quite daunted by the prospect too. Peer mentors provide information about these activities, the preparation for them, what to expect as well as how to get the most out of them. PAL sessions therefore include activities to help students prepare for the trip both from a physical 'what to pack' point of view and from a learning point of view of 'what you should know about in advance'. Mentees report that their mentors gave them the inside story and helped ensure they really made the best use of the experience. Mentors noted that this process helped them to revisit aspects of their course and their own field trip experiences raising new learning through potential application of subsequent topics covered. These mentors are also supported through regular debrief meetings with the programme organiser.

Example 3: Peer support for transition

All students have to transition into university life and study wherever they have come from. This process can be fraught with challenges, which can mean that a stressed or anxious student might withdraw from the university before the end of the first term. Having a university-wide peer support programme means that all students are offered assistance through this process. Peer mentors are assigned a group of new mentees possibly even prior to the start of term. This means they can make contact with their mentees and welcome them to the university in an informal and friendly manner. Mentees report that the psychological impact of merely knowing someone greatly reduces their anxiety, aids their confidence and helps them feel included. Mentors noted that this simple communication task was something they appreciated and found rewarding to offer to a new student. These mentors are offered occasional debrief meetings to feed back to the programme organiser and ask questions.

Delivery mediums for peer mentoring

Society has advanced in part due to the ongoing development of information and communication avenues. So while students did manage to maintain friendships and offer support to each other prior to the internet, mobile technology and social media sites, current peer programmes benefit from this wealth of modern communication channels. These might be categorised into:

- face-to-face (traditional classes and meetings)
- hard copy (traditional writing)
- online – virtual real time (synchronous, e.g. Skype, instant messaging)
- online – virtual 'recorded' (asynchronous, e.g. email, discussion forums, social media)
- telephone/mobile – real time (calls)
- telephone/mobile – delay response (texts).

People have their own preferences for communicating with friends, family, work colleagues and acquaintances. These communication avenues might differ depending on the group a person has been assigned to. You may prefer to call your family on the phone but opt to text friends and email work colleagues. The communication channel chosen for a peer programme might depend on several factors, such as physical proximity, access to the internet or mobile technology.

Peer programmes designed to support distance learning students make organising a physical face-to-face meet-up extremely difficult. Hence each peer programme must ascertain the best and most accessible channel of communication. Often campus-based peer programmes are structured using face-to-face meetings while distance learning groups utilise the internet to support their interaction. In practice, most peer programmes incorporate the use of more than one communication channel. The main thing to bear in mind here is that whatever approach is used it should be accessible to all participants. As a peer mentor, this might be something for you to discuss with your fellow mentors to ensure that the whole group will be accommodated. You may also consider the boundaries you wish to have in place concerning mentees contacting you. We will consider the various aspects of the role and its responsibilities and boundaries next.

Peer mentors – role, responsibilities and boundaries

Role

As a peer mentor you might view your role as a generally fairly straightforward activity of helping other students. However, the role is actually quite complex and you should be provided with some detailed and comprehensive training to ensure that you can meet the various challenges of the role. These challenges can be multidimensional, partly depending on the goals of the programme developer and partly depending on your own motivations and outlook.

The role involves a student providing guidance, support, advice and direction to other students in accordance with the programme's aims. These aims will direct the specifics of the role in extent, responsibilities, limitations and boundaries. You may wish to check the role description provided by your institution or programme organiser. It is important for you to be fully aware of the specific details of the role to avoid mistakes or unintentional consequences.

Responsibilities

In considering the wider implications of the role, it can be seen that it comes with significant responsibility. You are accountable for your own actions and decisions with respect to the programme, starting with your decision to take on the role and all it stands for. You will no doubt have had your reasons and a rationale underpinning this decision, which you may wish to reflect on at this point. It is worth noting that being responsible and accountable for something can be both empowering and frightening. To help you embrace this empowerment and minimise the potential challenges posed by this responsibility, it can be useful to break the role down into manageable sections or tasks. These are likely to fall under some common areas that relate to the most frequently cited responsibilities of peer mentors.

The common responsibilities for all peer mentors include:

- ensuring you are contactable by mentees via the agreed channel
- arranging peer meetings in accordance with the programme structure
- attending all meetings on time
- attending any compulsory training
- ensuring you are fully prepared for all meetings
- responding to mentees within a reasonable timeframe
- providing a supportive, fair, inclusive environment for mentees
- ensuring information provided is correct
- signposting to other services or tutors as appropriate
- maintaining records of peer meetings and activities as fits with the programme's aims and objectives
- taking part in debrief/feedback meetings with the programme organiser as arranged.

This is not intended as an exhaustive list of responsibilities. It would be wise to check with your particular programme organiser to ensure that you are aware of the specific requirements of your peer mentor role. These responsibilities are generally addressed during the peer mentor training, where you will be able to discuss the details of the responsibilities involved. For example, you may wish to check the details of arranging meetings: is it your responsibility to book a room, or will the organiser do that? It is often the logistics which are taken for granted but cause significant disruption to a programme's smooth operation if not attended to.

Boundaries

When we talk about boundaries we mean the limits of the role – where your role as a peer mentor ends and hence what peer leaders are generally not responsible for. The boundary might be seen as something you impose on your own role, and requests which fall outside this line should be refused. To visualise this, imagine a circle drawn around you as a peer mentor, much in the same way as you might have a fence around your house. Everything inside the circle is your responsibility, while everything outside the circle is outside your remit and is someone else's responsibility. The line of the circle itself is your boundary. However, this is a somewhat grey hazy line where some items may or may not fall within your remit. The requests that fall within this grey area should be checked with your programme organiser before you attempt to deal with them. If you are concerned about confidentiality you may wish to pose the 'what if' question to your programme organiser. You could ask: 'If I had a mentee or student ask me … what should I do?'

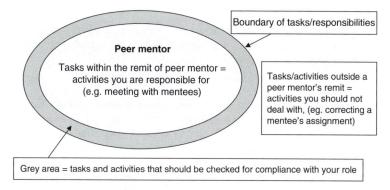

The peer mentor remit circle

The circle represents your role and all it entails – this is where all tasks and activities sit and it connects closely with your responsibilities. This might include meeting with your mentees on a regular basis, offering support, facilitating discussion, signposting to university services and all aspects as identified by your peer programme organiser. Outside this circle is where activities that do not come under your role sit. This might include proofreading mentees' work, checking mentees' assignment references, offering crisis counselling and directing mentees in answering assignments. You may well be asked by mentees to undertake some of these tasks, so it is important to explain your role and its boundaries at one of your earliest meetings. There is more discussion of boundaries in Chapter 6.

Embracing diversity within mentoring

Most universities are diverse places, welcoming students from all over the globe, from all walks of life and with highly varied backgrounds. Hence diversity relates not only to people from different cultures but also to those who might be of a different age range, have a physical or mental health condition, or come from a non-traditional route into university. Many universities have traditionally received the majority of intakes of students from particular groups of people in society. This has been changing for some time, with a much broader intake of students seen in most universities today. As well as the student population, the staff demographic is changing, with many more staff being recruited from across the globe from a wide variety of backgrounds. To recognise and support this development, many universities now have equality and diversity policies which connect with government acts, such as the UK Equality Act 2010.

Activity 2.5

Equality and diversity

Are you aware of your university's policies relating to equality and diversity? If not, now would be a good time to look them up and perhaps use them as a basis for a discussion with your mentees or fellow mentors.

Universities have developed to provide communities of learning where people come together to share, discuss and debate all manner of topics in a safe environment. To enhance and support this community of learning ethos, many universities have instigated a strategy to promote integration and cohesion. Part of this strategy is activities that encourage and support transition, learning and studying together. Peer programmes are a key part of the strategy. They offer a welcoming, inclusive forum where students can interact without staff present but with the support and framework of the university structure. This is an opportunity for you as a peer mentor to engage with developing inclusive practices in your own and others' activities.

Getting to know students with differing backgrounds, values, cultural practices and views is an important developmental experience. It helps to break down negative perceptions and skewed understandings of other groups of people. Our perceptions of others are influenced by many factors, such as the media, fictional portrayals through TV or books, and advertising. The views of those persons who are important in our lives, such as our family and friends, are also significant factors in our perceptions of others. Gaining an understanding of other groups of people in this way can obviously lead to severe misconceptions, which is why it is so important to keep an open mind when meeting new people. As a peer mentor this is especially important and you will no doubt receive training which will highlight this.

Some peer mentoring programmes are designed to aid transition into university. This is especially important where students join the university from another country. As a peer mentor in this case it is imperative that you meet with the mentees and find out who they are and let them come to know you. Helping them to understand the culture and traditions of your country and learning about theirs will help break down barriers and make them feel included and valued as individuals. Remember, though, that your mentees might have also been influenced by others, so it may take repeated efforts to establish trust.

Similarly, people of other groups will need support to help them feel included and valued. Being able to understand and appreciate the challenges faced by others is a crucial skill of peer mentors. Students with caring responsibilities, for example, will face different challenges. These issues can be quite easily appreciated and supported. However, it can be quite difficult to understand the often hidden issues presented by other groups. You will therefore need to try to be quite perceptive about their feelings, concerns, anxieties, etc. in order to help them integrate with the student cohort you are supporting.

Activity 2.6

Transition and integration

Think of a time when you have been in a minority group.

- How did it make you feel?
- How did you handle it?
- What can you do to support students who are in a minority?

The main thing to remember is to keep an open mind, be welcoming to all, and try to appreciate and empathise with the challenges faced by your mentees.

Conclusion

This chapter has introduced you to the various aspects of the role of peer mentor and the place of peer mentoring in universities. As a peer mentor you play a vital part in a number of university strategies to address retention, achievement, equality and diversity. This is done through offering your mentees support, guidance and signposting to other university services. As we have seen, there are various models by which this is put into practice, from quite structured approaches to more informal arrangements. Regardless of the model adopted, all stakeholders can benefit from the experience, including you as a peer mentor. The extent to which you benefit from this experience depends largely on what you put into it. The subsequent chapters in this book will help you realise these gains.

Key points from this chapter

- The specifics of the peer mentoring role depend on the goals of the peer programme.
- Peer mentoring supports a number of university overarching goals and strategies.

- Peer mentors should maintain an open-minded, welcoming, inclusive and supportive approach.
- Peer mentors are role models for students at earlier stages of study.

Further sources of information

- Your own and other university peer support/learning webpages.

Why Become a Peer Mentor?

By the end of this chapter you will:

- have an awareness of the psychology of mentoring
- have a clear understanding of your motives for becoming a peer mentor
- be aware of the benefits of becoming a peer mentor
- know how to develop and enhance your emotional intelligence by becoming a peer mentor
- be able to create your mentor profile.

Chapter 2 introduced you to the role of peer mentoring in university. With that information in mind, it is useful to examine your motivation for becoming a peer mentor before you make the decision to join a mentoring scheme. Helping others through mentoring can be enormously satisfying, but doing so does not always have to be a purely selfless act.

This chapter will look at the psychology of mentoring and ask why people choose to help others. It will also consider the more subjective aspects of the mentoring role and ask you to reflect on your motivations and expectations in a personal rather than an academic or professional sense (these will be covered in Chapter 8).

The psychology of mentoring

Helping others is an everyday occurrence and one that comes naturally to most people, but have you ever stopped to consider why this is? What is it about human beings that makes us willing to help each other, often without stopping to think? The simple answer is that it is a learned behaviour. As children, we receive praise for being 'nice' and are chastised for being 'selfish'. It is little wonder then that when an opportunity arises to help people who are facing the same difficult situation that we once faced, we want to help.

The definition of 'helping' is doing something that results in some benefit to or improves the wellbeing of another person, but it can also have a detrimental effect on the helper. Mentoring involves hard work on the part of the mentor and it may not always be appreciated. When you first become a mentor, despite all the information that may have been provided, you may not fully realise the extent of the time and effort required because your relationship with your mentee(s) is not yet established. Once you actually get started, you may find that you experience unexpected frustration and possibly disappointment. You will of course undergo training that explores issues such as boundaries, expectations and potential problems, but, until the process begins, the full implications of these matters may not be apparent.

While the role of mentor is extremely worthwhile and rewarding, it is also important to be realistic about what is expected of you (see Chapter 4 for more on this). It can be a challenging and time-consuming task and should not be entered into lightly. So stop for a minute and think a little more deeply about why you might choose, or have chosen, to become a mentor. Your underlying motives are often complex and there is likely to be an element of self-interest (Schroeder et al., 1995).

Activity 3.1

Think back to when you first heard that your programme of study had a mentoring scheme and needed new mentors.

What was your initial reaction? Perhaps you immediately volunteered? Perhaps you wanted to wait until you knew more about it? If you signed up without thinking, did you later have any concerns about the role? What were they? If you are yet to volunteer, what else do you want to know before you enrol?

Reasons to consider mentoring

If you are new to mentoring, perhaps you were asked to sign up by your tutor. If this is the case, you were no doubt pleased that they considered you a good candidate and enjoyed the positive recognition. If you are responding to a general request for volunteers, perhaps you want to learn new skills to enhance your CV.

If you are already mentoring at university, or in another context, think back to when you first got involved. Your first encounter with peer mentoring may have been as a mentee. Perhaps you had a positive experience and want to replicate this for another student. If this is the case, ask yourself why? When you were a mentee, did you wonder about the motivations and feelings of your mentor? How do you think that giving the same help to another student, as a mentor, will benefit *you*?

A survey of new peer mentors carried out at the University of Kent in 2015 revealed that, in the initial stages, students had a number of reasons for becoming a mentor. The majority of students were motivated, at least in part, by the desire to help others.

Activity 3.2

What are your reasons for wanting to become a peer mentor? Rank them in order of importance.

1.

2.

3.

4.

5.

Positive experience as a mentee

For some the decision to mentor others came as a result of their own experience. Those who had a positive experience of being a mentee wanted to replicate this. The following quotations are taken from student mentors at a UK university:

> I had a mentor myself in my first year, and she was very helpful. I want to help out as well.

> I was a mentee last year when I was in my second year of the course. Whilst being a mentee I had a positive experience, where my mentors were able to help me in both personal and academic ways.

Negative experience as a mentee

In some cases the experience of being a mentee was not a positive one and so students wanted to do better:

> I was very lost last year as my mentor was not at all helpful and there came times when I needed reassurance. I believe this is something I can give my mentees.

> My mentor was okay, but he was not always around when I needed him. I'm going to be more organised.

Offering support to other students

Other students became mentors because they wanted to give students what they wished had been available to them:

> I wanted to help those with problems similar to what I faced in the first year, to help get the best out of the mentees and give them the confidence to progress.

> I became a mentor to help the younger year not make some of the same mistakes I did. I had a mentor and they were very helpful so I wanted to replicate that with someone else, to guide them through the year and make the course easier and approachable.

> I wanted to help advise and guide students below me the way I wished I could have been, inform them about what they have ahead of them. Let them know how to keep on top of everything and be a support system.

> It was about being able to give first years some guidance in their first year of university. I wanted to become the person that I needed when I was younger, to give reassuring advice.

> In hindsight I know I stressed too much over things last year – I can reassure students that it's not actually as horrifying as it seems.

However, helping others can also be very satisfying on a more personal level. This was recognised by new mentors when they commented why they signed up to be a mentor:

> For the satisfaction of knowing I could have potentially helped someone.

> To prove to myself that my knowledge is worth passing on to others.

> To meet people and extend my social relationships.

> Because I think it will be a challenge and therefore a useful experience that will help make me a better student as well.

> To challenge myself. Keep myself at the top of the game.

In addition to wanting to help others, new mentors also recognised that joining the scheme would be useful in terms of their own academic progression:

> It will give me the opportunity to revisit topics I learnt in my first and second years.

> To learn what I already know – I will realise what my skills are when I talk to others.

> To allow me to re-cover areas from my previous year that may aid me.

> I'll learn creativity from them as they're still not in the mindset of being restricted by planning rules.

The advantages of being a mentor were also seen as going beyond university life and a useful way of preparing for the workplace:

> It's a good thing to have on your CV and the skills acquired during the scheme will help me out in my future career.

I am interested in a career in teaching.

Mentoring will improve my confidence and leadership skills in future.

I want to improve my employability and have an extra thing to put on my CV once leaving university.

I want to work at a university (research and teaching) and I think this will be a good way to see if I enjoy this kind of work. Also, it is the most relevant thing to put on my CV as I want to go into an academic career.

As you can see, there are many reasons to become a peer mentor; it is not only about helping other people. By becoming a mentor you are given an opportunity to develop your employability skills, such as leadership and group work. Your improved communication skills will raise your self-confidence and benefit you in your academic development. Going over topics will consolidate your knowledge base of core issues and elements in your course, so you are likely to see an improvement in your own academic performance. Your mentoring experience could also give you the edge over competitors when it comes to getting a job. Not only will you be able to compile a much more attractive CV but you will also be able to improve your communication skills for use in an interview situation.

Know yourself

Being a mentor puts you in a position of responsibility and changes your status within the student body and the university as a whole. You will no longer be simply a 'student' but part of the establishment, forming a link between fellow students and the faculty staff. The nature of the mentor–mentee relationship also puts the mentor, to some extent, in a position of power because help and resources tend to flow in one direction. This creates the possibility of misunderstandings, which may cause problems (Colvin and Ashman, 2010). Any suggestion, whether explicit or implicit, that the mentor is better or more important than the mentee must be avoided so that both mentor and mentee get the most from the relationship. After all, you are both students, you just happen to be at different stages of your studies. Your mentee, however, may feel intimidated by someone with more experience and knowledge.

You may find that being in this rather unique position prompts a re-evaluation of the way in which you approach and react to certain situations. It is essential therefore that you take time to reflect on your motives for becoming a mentor and are realistic about the expectations you have of yourself and your mentees. As a mentor you have the advantage of experience. You know what it is like to have been at an earlier stage in your studies and perhaps you made mistakes. Ideally you will pass on this knowledge and experience, and your mentee will listen attentively and act accordingly. But you can also remember how it felt to be a new student. Your priorities and concerns may well have been different from what they are now, so try to bear this in mind. Remember that if your mentee does not attend an arranged meeting, this may be impolite but it is not personal. Ask yourself whether you bother to email your lecturer in advance if you cannot make the lecture or seminar? There are other potential problems, including miscommunication, lack of engagement and blurring the boundaries of the role. We will look at troubleshooting and potential problems in Chapter 7. For now, though, as you work through the remainder of this chapter, bear in mind that as well as considering your own motives and capabilities, you will need to consider those of your mentees.

As a mentor you will be expected to:

- **Be positive:** Your mentees may lack confidence in their ability to study or be lacking in academic skills. You can help lift the spirits of these students. This requires good listening skills, often listening 'between the lines' to what is not said, picking up on body language and responding in a clear, positive way while at the same time being empathetic to your mentee's situation.
- **Be a good listener**: Be empathetic rather than sympathetic and encourage your mentees to see that you respect their views.
- **Be reliable:** Set the standard in the relationship by committing to and arranging regular meetings and not making promises that you cannot keep. It is likely that you will communicate with your mentees electronically rather than face to face. Because this means that your conversations will not have the advantage of facial expression or tone of voice, it is important to be careful in the way you word your initial messages and your responses. Always be aware that what is 'heard' by your mentee may not be the same as what was 'said' by you as you were writing it.
- **Show interest:** Make a conscious effort to remember previous discussions so that the first part of any meeting reviews the last session. Keeping records of meetings will make your mentees feel valued. In doing this you are communicating your genuine interest in the wellbeing of your mentees, making them feel valued. This will enhance the effectiveness of the relationship.
- **Be approachable:** Try to be relaxed, friendly and responsive to the needs and concerns expressed by your mentees. Once they have the confidence to talk to you about issues of concern, potential 'mountains' will remain 'molehills'.
- **Be non-judgemental:** Try not to apply your own standards and experiences as a template for the relationship. Your mentees will have different life experiences and different pressures to cope with. The tone and speed of your voice can be very telling. If you speak quickly, your mentees may feel that they are taking up too much of your time and that they cannot ask further questions. Interrupting may indicate that what a mentee is saying has no value, or that you consider them to be asking stupid questions. While it is fine to prompt if your mentee is struggling to articulate what they mean, it is important to be patient and know when you should wait and allow them the time to finish.
- **Be realistic:** There will be goals or standards that you aim for in the relationship, but be aware that goals can only be achieved once a rapport has been established. Any goals set can be broken down into achievable targets.
- **Be aware:** Your mentees may not always be organised. At school, young people are sometimes used to having their lives organised for them, and are not used to making appointments or arrangements for themselves. It is your job to encourage the development of this skill in your mentees.

- **Be honest:** As in other areas of your life, there will be people who do not gel and find it difficult to get along with each other. If you find that the relationship with your mentees is uncomfortable or not working, this is not a reflection on you. You should recognise when this becomes an issue and seek advice from your school.
- **Communicate clearly:** Explain your intentions to mentees, discuss their expectations, and check your understanding and theirs. This might be done face to face or electronically. Either way, it is important to use clear, unambiguous language to confirm each party's understanding of the discussion and decide on the next step as appropriate.
- **Be inclusive:** There is likely to be a diverse range of people within your group in terms of ethnicity, faith, socio-economic background, age, ability and learning preference. You can create an inclusive atmosphere by speaking clearly for mentees with English as a second language; avoiding stereotyping; making sure that the discussion is open to the whole group but listening to each group member and having some topics for discussion in reserve in case you need to steer the conversation in a different direction.

As you have seen, in terms of your own approach and ability, being a mentor can be emotionally challenging, and at times even a bit daunting. You will probably find that any areas of concern you may have will be covered by your training, but before you sign up it is useful to reflect on the personal skills that are needed for the role so that you are aware of any areas that you may wish to work on or find out more about. You may also wish to think about the way in which you can set the tone for how the mentoring partnership develops by being aware of your own behaviour and the way in which it is received by your mentees. There is more about emotional intelligence in Chapter 6.

In a mentoring relationship you will be called upon to face a variety of situations. Sometimes you will be confident and handle them with ease, but there may be times when you do not know the answers to questions your mentees ask, or how to react to particular circumstances. Mentees will assume that you have all the answers. Most of the time you will, but there may be times when you are unsure or uncomfortable. This is absolutely fine; you are not expected to be able to solve all the issues that mentees raise. Your job is to enable them to find the answers, and sometimes this may involve looking for those answers together. This is the time when you will call upon, and develop, your emotional intelligence.

Your mentoring profile

Once you have undergone your training, you may be asked to write your mentor profile, your personal brand, to be sent out to mentees or to go on the school website. This is a chance for you to showcase your skills both within the university and, potentially, to future employers, and to create your personal brand. Jeff Bezos, the founder of Amazon.com, describes a personal brand as 'what people say about you when you leave the room'.

Activity 3.3

Here are four examples. Look at each one in turn and think about what sort of person the mentor in question appears to be. Which one of these would you choose to be your mentor and why?

- Hi. I have completed two years of higher education so I understand the giant leap in requirements from A level to degree level. You will mostly find me in the library and I will always be happy to help in any way I can, whether it's educational or what night is best to go out. I am happy and friendly, and a good listener, and would be happy to tell you about any aspect of university life. I look forward to meeting you.

- I feel my role is to be a general help to you if needed with any struggles you may be facing such as essays, referencing (which you most likely will need help with if you are like me) or just generally adjusting to the subject or uni life! Please don't feel scared or embarrassed to ask me literally anything, I'm always around on campus and am here as much or as little as needed! I look forward to meeting you.

- I am a part-time mature student in the second part of my final year. I am well aware of the varied calls on a mature student's time, with conflicts of interests, so time management is the key to staying sane. The first year can be daunting for any new student, but particularly as a mature student. Don't worry, though – your co-students will be accepting. I can help with how to get the most out of your time at university – referencing, seminars and the value of reading! If you are ever in doubt about something, please feel free to ask. I am here to help.

- I will be one of your mentors for the following year. I feel my role is to guide and advise you in any way you need. So essays, referencing, adjusting to university life and whatever else you might be worried about. I'm here to help. Feel free to ask me anything (no matter how small) at any time I'll always be available and on campus, no doubt in the library! I look forward to meeting you!

When it comes to creating your own profile, you should start by asking yourself a number of key questions. In order to answer them, you might like to review the previous activities included in this chapter. Then ask yourself:

- Why did I become a mentor?
- What do I expect to achieve from the role?
- What can I give to the role?
- What are my strengths and weaknesses?
- How do I want others to view me?

Activity 3.4

Jot down the answers to the questions above and create a draft profile. Be sure to emphasise your skills and commitment to the role and say something about why you chose to join the scheme.

Conclusion

This chapter has outlined the psychology of mentoring as a helping activity which comes naturally to some people. It has also summarised a number of different reasons for becoming a peer mentor from a selfless act of generosity to a more instrumental motivation to improve one's own skills and CV. It is useful for you to reflect on your motivations for becoming a mentor and to realise that you may have multiple reasons, and these reasons may change over time.

It is widely recognised that mentoring can help with the development of a number of transferable skills that are valued by employers (Eldridge and Wilson, 2003; Norris et al., 2006). As a mentor your training and experience will give you a greater sense of self-awareness and emotional intelligence, which will be highly regarded by future employers.

The final part of this chapter encouraged you to think about your own mentoring profile as a way to initiate engagement with your mentees and as a form of personal branding which will have application beyond your time as a mentor.

Key points from this chapter

- There are a wide range of motivations for becoming a mentor.
- Mentoring develops your self-awareness and emotional intelligence.
- As a mentor you will develop an awareness of how others perceive you.

What Characteristics Are Needed to Be an Effective Peer Mentor?

By the end of this chapter you will:

- have an overview of the optimal characteristics for peer mentors
- have an understanding of the meaning of what these characteristics are
- have an appreciation of the impact of these characteristics on mentoring
- have a range of exercises and examples exemplifying the impact of different characteristics to compare to your own experience.

This chapter considers the characteristics of effective peer mentors. There are a number of attributes and qualities which are desirable for peer mentors to possess so that they connect well with their mentees as well as their fellow mentors. This results in an effective mentoring relationship which is crucial in meeting the goals of the peer programme. It is these attributes and qualities of effective peer mentors that we will consider within this chapter.

You will find that mentoring can be a fun and rewarding experience which often has a profound effect on both mentor and mentee. Ensuring that this effect is a positive one for all concerned is one of the main goals of programme organisers and why they often spend significant amounts of time recruiting those that they feel are the right mentors for their programme. It has been recognised that the successfulness of a peer programme is very much in the hands of the mentors (Keenan and Benjamin, 2012), so attracting the right mentors is crucial. The question is: What is the 'right kind of mentor'? Do you need to have the right kind of characteristics before embarking on the role, or can these qualities be taught and learnt?

Which type of mentoring is right for me?

You will find that your role as a peer mentor is extensive and varied, and this makes it both interesting and a challenge. When you consider the types of mentor characteristic that are appropriate for optimal effectiveness, you also need to take into account the type of programme you may be involved in. The different programme models might be seen as needing a slightly different approach to mentoring where strength in certain characteristics may be helpful. It is possibly obvious that a programme with a bias towards transition support will need mentors with good campus knowledge, while one designed to aid subject understanding will require mentors with good comprehension of that topic. However, the situation is not quite as simple as that. As a peer mentor you will find yourself confronted with students asking for help in all matters from aspects of study to concerns about loneliness regardless of the peer programme's overall goals. It will not come as a surprise, therefore, in view of the broad role of the peer mentor, that the attributes needed to be effective in this position are similarly quite extensive. Hence, while the different models of peer programme somewhat dictate the ideal attributes, with perhaps empathy being pivotal in pastoral-oriented programmes or a propensity for group management in study session-style programmes, the wider remit of the role demands consideration of a broader array of characteristics. In your role as a peer mentor you will find that your natural characteristics help you in some instances, whereas in other situations you may be less comfortable. Don't worry about this, but be aware of when you are more, or less, comfortable as it will add to your own learning and development. It is only when you are able to identify situations that align with your attributes and those that pose a challenge, that you can start to ascertain which characteristics to improve so that you can deal with the challenges with more confidence. We will look at how to enhance various characteristics later in the chapter.

Activity 4.1

Identify experiences where you have not been completely comfortable and consider why this was in terms of your characteristics. For example, you may not have been comfortable in a large group of people you did not know as you are not confident about approaching strangers.

Identifying effective characteristics

Obviously, being a peer mentor places you in a sort of leadership position where you lead your mentees through your advice and guidance. While there have been relatively few studies investigating the characteristics of effective peer mentors in higher education, there are many which examine the attributes of leaders in other situations. These have most notably been conducted in business settings and the military, where effective leadership is connected to tangible real-world results. The feeling is that wars have been won and businesses have attained global success in part due to the person at the helm.

Hence the business world considers leadership to be pivotal in its success. As such, many large corporations include psychometric testing as part of the recruitment process to try to identify the person with the optimal characteristics for their company. You may experience such tests in your future job-hunting activities. However, while psychometric tests might seem useful, research appears to indicate that a combination of characteristics applied in appropriate ways commensurate with the situation at hand is the real key to success. So everyone has some characteristics that make them good mentors when those characteristics are applied in the right ways for a given situation. Offering empathy to a mentee who is anxious due to loneliness will likely be much more effective than providing organisational skills support.

Activity 4.2

Have a look on the internet for psychometric tests and try one or two of these (there are numerous free online psychometric tests). What do you feel the results tell you about yourself?

Generally, peer mentor recruitment in higher education has not taken on the approach of personality profiling, but studies such as those reviewed by Terrion and Leonard (2007) indicate the desire to find suitable characteristics that result in effective mentoring. You may be asked to complete a personality questionnaire as part of the selection and training process, the most common of which is arguably the Myers–Briggs Type Indicator first published in the 1940s. Undertaking a personality test can be an interesting exercise that offers some insights into your characteristics, although it should not be relied upon for clinical measures. Its true usefulness might be seen as guiding your training and development via reflection on the results. Undertaking such a test will help you to identify aspects where you are less confident, which you can then plan to enhance through training and developmental activities.

Terrion and Leonard's (2007) review of literature pertaining to mentor descriptors found that, in addition to some fundamental aspects, there were ten key characteristics common to successful mentoring. They assigned these to two groups:

- Career-related function
    Programme of study
    Self-enhancement motivation
- Psychosocial function
    Communication skills
    Supportiveness
    Trustworthiness
    Interdependent attitude to mentoring, mentees and programme staff
    Empathy
    Personality match with mentees
    Enthusiasm
    Flexibility

A number of these aspects are under your control, such as self-motivation and communication skills. However, various aspects of the career and psychosocial functions are thought to be part of a person's innate character. Whether these are controllable and hence changeable or adjustable is questionable, and we will consider this later in this chapter.

Emotional intelligence and effective mentors

Understanding these seemingly innate characteristics might be addressed by looking at your own emotional intelligence. Goleman (1996) views effective emotional intelligence as the ability to know oneself and others with respect to feelings, thoughts and actions. As you might expect, having an appreciation of how you react yourself is key to developing effective approaches to understanding and dealing with other people. This crucial skill is fundamental to effective peer mentoring. Your role as a peer mentor is to interact with your peers, so being able to predict and respond appropriately to their reactions to the experience will ensure your success in this role. Getting to know yourself is pivotal in gaining effective skills for mentoring. Generally, people know how they tend to react in various situations. For example, you may think of yourself as extroverted if you tend to feel comfortable talking to strangers. However, what may be less clear is what impact your approach has on others. Correctly gauging and assessing a person's reaction is not a straightforward task as it requires a high level of sensitivity from sound observational skills. These observations might comprise facial expressions, body language, voice tone and modulation, verbal communication content, etc. Information can also be acquired through written communication, cooperation and organisational activities. Face-to-face observations can sometimes make it easier to classify whether a person is happy/sad, angry/calm, etc. The other avenues pose more of a challenge with perhaps the seeming dissatisfaction that might result from an email or the possible misinterpretation arising out of non-participation. We have all probably received an email which seemed to us a little unfriendly, unkind or even rude, but later we found out that this was not the intention of the author at all. This is perhaps a good reason to always check the intention before jumping to conclusions. Similarly, a mentee might not be participating in the session for a wide variety of reasons. It is not necessarily that they are unhappy with the session per se, but that they are experiencing something in their lives which is making it less easy for them to participate. Non-participation in activities is often a sign of stress or depression, which you should bear in mind. Hence the key is to correctly understand your mentees' situation, thinking and the reasons for their behaviour. This applies to understanding not only your mentees' drivers but also your own. As you no doubt appreciate, the ability to do this is an important characteristic for effective peer mentors.

Being an inspirational mentor

Mentors, like leaders, come in many guises, but it might be said that there is a fundamental difference between a good mentor who inspires and a mentor who just directs. Directive-type leaders are often found where quite a rigid structure prevails, where leadership is objective and results are quantifiable. These leaders do not seek or want input from their subordinates; they just want them to follow instructions. There is no discussion or flexibility. Conversely, being inspirational is probably more of an art and possibly part of someone's character. We can perhaps all remember teachers, mentors, authors, coaches, or family members who inspired an interest in something within us. This may have led to keen participation in a hobby, influenced educational choices or resulted in a particular perspective. These people who influenced our lives did not necessarily have a particular goal in mind, they did not set out to convert us to their thinking. So what was it that this inspirational person did, said or wrote that created this result? Such influence often stems from their own intense interest in something. Being highly motivated by something tends to make us keen to share that enthusiasm, thereby generating interest and passion in others. Generally, as a mentor, your goals will be those of the peer programme, so the key will be for you to achieve these goals by inspiring your mentees rather than directing them. Ideally you will enthuse your mentees in the chosen area by putting forward attractive and beneficial avenues or options. So, for example, as a peer mentor you might aim to motivate your mentees to learn and understand the topic of your peer programme, and you might inspire this interest partly by being enthusiastic about the topic yourself. As you might guess, being a good, effective mentor encompasses a raft of characteristics from enthusiasm and supportiveness to communication and flexibility. When these are pulled together the result is an inspiring mentor whose mentees are eager to follow and listen to them. Developing an inspirational approach to mentoring requires consideration of the associated characteristics and a willingness to embrace them. First, you will find it useful to ascertain what your natural characteristics are. You can then use these to provide a basis for enhancing the pertinent characteristics that will enable you to become a more inspirational mentor.

Activity 4.3

What do you think the qualities of an inspirational mentor are? To what extent do you believe you have some of these qualities and how might you develop others?

How do I know what my characteristics are?

Finding out what your own characteristics are can be an enlightening activity. However, a word of caution – tests to ascertain a person's characteristics are never 100% reliable. There are a number of factors which influence the outcome, from the individual's mood at the time of taking the test to their comprehension and interpretation of the questions.

There are of course numerous free personality tests on the internet which may go some way to identifying your own characteristics. Many of the online tests are based around commonalities of the major personality tests including the Myers–Briggs Type Indicator and The Big Five Personality Test. However, in taking these tests, try to be aware of what situations and experiences run through your mind as you answer the questions. People often act differently according to the situation they find themselves in. You may be quite confident and outgoing in one aspect of your life but lack confidence in another, making you hesitant and perhaps shy. Answering the personality test questions in relation to such situations will likely bias your answers, hence you might wish to complete the tests more than once when you are in differing frames of mind. For example, complete a test when you are feeling generally confident, when perhaps you have had a good, productive and positive situation, and then again when you have had an experience where you were not confident and did not feel it went well. You can then compare your results and see if there is a difference, which will help you appreciate the influence of a situation on your mental state and perhaps overall personality. This will also aid you in understanding the importance of preparing appropriately for your peer sessions so that you are confident in what you will do and how you will deliver them.

Activity 4.4

Search on the internet for a selection of personality tests. Undertake at least two of these, noting your emotional state and focus of attention at the time. Retake these same tests a few days or weeks later when you are in a different state of mind with a different focus of attention. Compare the results. How similar are your results?

Characteristics self-review

While it is beyond the scope of this book to devise a psychological assessment of personality, we can pose some questions and statements to aid consideration and self-review of personal characteristics.

Complete the characteristics review table in the Appendix. Try not to overthink your answers but use your initial gut reaction to each statement to decide on your rating. The usefulness of any self-evaluation questionnaire is in how it helps you think about yourself and your situation. As such it is important to be completely honest with yourself as you respond to each statement.

Ideally you should complete this questionnaire more than once on different days and at different times. Try to choose days and times when you know you tend to feel differently, such as just before a break when you're feeling a little upbeat, or when you're feeling less positive, such as when you have several assignments to write. Once you have completed this, review your responses and consider how these vary on your different test days. Are they the same or very similar, or are there distinct differences?

As part of your reflection on this exercise, consider the questionnaire and your answers to the statements with regard to:

- what influenced your answers
- how you interpreted the statements
- what frame of mind you were in while completing the review
- what your focus of attention was, and what experiences or memories you drew on to respond to the statements.

Consider your outcomes as you read through the next section and decide which characteristics you would like to enhance. You might also wish to consider whether this would be a useful exercise to do with your mentees. If so, what would you hope that you and they would get out of it? Be careful to ensure that this is a constructive and beneficial exercise where there is discussion of the positive aspects of all characteristics. You might need to permit them to keep their answers to themselves and use it as a purely reflective activity to identify potential aspects for development via the peer programme.

Can 'good' characteristics be learnt?

The premise that characteristics can be learnt relies on the supposition that these 'good' characteristics are a product of nurture rather than nature. That is, they are not necessarily innate, genetically inherited, fundamental and unchanging parts of personality; they are an adaptable ingredient. To a certain extent, all characteristics are adaptable if people wish to make changes to themselves. The key here is willingness and enthusiasm to change. We perhaps all know someone who has changed themselves in some way; possibly not a major change but a significant one, at least for them. The question is whether this is learning or something else. In making the change you may well learn about aspects of yourself, but this is possibly not learning in the traditional sense. Designing learning activities for the development of desirable characteristics will be less of a teaching process and perhaps more aligned to helping you fully understand and appreciate the impact of this on your skills and effectiveness not only as a peer mentor but for all aspects of your life. Generally this learning process might take the form of observation, case study review, personal accounts, scenario activities and practice with a bias of these depending on the particular characteristic in question. The next section considers the individual attributes listed by Terrion and Leonard as ideal peer mentor psychosocial characteristics and suggests potential developmental strategies for each.

Communication skills

Communication incorporates both verbal and non-verbal communication through a variety of mediums. The oral, verbal, audio spoken word can be transmitted not only in face-to-face communications but also via electronic means such as telephones where no visual cues are possible. Similarly, using mediums such as text or email offering only non-oral communication risks misinterpretation as you have no doubt experienced yourself. These mediums often pose an obstacle to good communication and require careful consideration as to how to overcome this challenge. Ideally your oral communication should be clear and appropriate for the situation. This might mean keeping it light-hearted when getting to know your mentees, but more sombre when a mentee has conveyed something emotionally difficult for them. Being clear in your oral communication takes thought and practice. Hearing someone tell you of an emotionally difficult situation can often feel embarrassing or uncomfortable, and many people tend to react in a sort of laughing, jovial manner. Obviously this does not help the mentee and can make them feel stupid or belittled. Hence practising your reaction to hearing this type of subject is very important. A significant aspect to this and to good communication generally is good listening skills, both actual and demonstrated. Listening shows you care and will enhance confidence and trust. Actual listening ensures that you know what is being said, and demonstrated listening ensures that your mentee feels that you are listening to them. Demonstrated listening can be through facial expressions, body language, appropriate noises (hmms, etc.), paraphrasing at the end, etc.

Communication skills can be taught and learnt but must be taken in and fully adopted in order to make this part of your character. This takes a good deal of practice and perhaps a change in approach if it's new to you. However, as one of the most important mentor characteristics reported by mentees, it is obviously worth the effort.

Case scenario: A mentor arrives late and flustered to a peer meeting. On arrival they begin by giving excuses for their lateness and blaming it on others. A mentee wishes to raise a concern that they are quite worried about. However, the mentor is distracted by their own efforts to excuse their lateness and does not pay close attention to what the mentee is saying. The mentor fails to understand the mentee's concerns and just tells them not to worry, moving the conversation on to a light general social chat. The mentee feels awkward and ceases speaking.

The mentee's situation is not dealt with and they feel let down and dissatisfied with their mentor.

You might wish to consider how you might deal with this situation and/or what advice you would give to this mentor.

Supportiveness

An encouraging and caring attitude goes a long way towards making your mentees feel supported. You will need to ascertain what type of support your mentees need and want. You will also need to bear in mind that the way that this is provided is just as important. You need to make clear that you are highly willing to help them but that there are boundaries. Also fundamental to good mentoring is your interest in assisting them to help themselves. Empowering mentees to become more independent learners and members of the student community will result in much better outcomes for your mentees, both academically and personally. You can facilitate this process by supporting your mentees in considering the issues and working through possible solutions to find something that works for them. Being supportive is not just doing things for your mentees; it is about helping them to find or work out the means to answer their own questions. Mentees frequently ask their mentors about assignments as they are often stressed when they feel they don't know where to start, so supporting them in discussing possible avenues to ascertain a way forward is highly beneficial. They can then use this approach for their subsequent assignments, which will help to reduce their anxiety and aid their academic skills development.

Being supportive with personal issues is quite tricky. Mentees need to feel you care about them as individuals and care about how they feel. Demonstrating a caring and supportive approach does not mean you have to sort out their personal issues though. Listening to them and perhaps signposting them to the appropriate service is the best avenue. Often just listening to them is enough; it is common to need to share a concern before being ready to move on. The main thing for mentees is that you take an active interest in them and their issues. Taking brief notes during meetings can be very useful in enabling you to remember what you've discussed previously so that you can follow it up at subsequent meetings.

Training to be supportive, encouraging and caring is obviously not a straightforward task. Your developmental activities to enhance these aspects could take the form of scenario exercises, reflection activities, observation of other mentors and people involved in caring professions, etc. It is unlikely that you will learn to be encouraging and caring from reading a text, although this may offer some ideas for appropriate language and communication avenues. Discussion with your fellow mentors about how each of you deals with these types of issue will give you some additional ideas and a wider array of strategies for supporting your mentees.

As you might guess, mentees are very grateful to mentors they feel made a difference to their student experience through their support efforts. Not only will your personal approach to supporting your mentees reap benefits for them but also you will learn about the importance of a caring attitude when dealing with others. This will help you in all your future interactions with people, both personally and professionally.

Case scenario: A new group of mentees is given a tour of the library by their mentor. The mentor points out the sections which are specifically useful for their topic area. They demonstrate the use of the online library search systems for journal articles and explain how to make use of Boolean operators. At a later meeting the mentor gets the mentees to look at their assignment brief and come up with key terms for a literature search using the library's databases. The mentor then assists the mentees in undertaking a focused database search.

The mentees felt supported in their studies not only for the current period but also for the future. The mentees realised that the library search skills developed through this exercise would be valuable throughout their whole course.

You may wish to think back to how you found using the library when you first started your course. How did you find out which databases to use? How did you come up with effective key terms for use in searching databases?

Trustworthiness

Peer programmes are generally offered to mentees as a safe place to discuss issues and concerns they may have. However, they are unlikely to do this if they do not feel that they can trust their mentor. Developing trust takes time in any relationship, whether that's with new friends or in a peer programme. Mentees need to feel that their mentor will maintain confidentiality with the information imparted and that they are reliable in this. This is crucial to the mentor–mentee relationship and, once broken, such trust will be extremely difficult to regain. Maintaining a high level of integrity and a professional approach is paramount.

Gaining someone's trust requires significant time and effort from you in the same way as it would in making new friends that you grow to trust and who develop trust in you. Often a sharing of personal experiences helps in this respect as it feels more like a two-way mutual development of trust as you both share personal information. This is not to say that as a mentor you should divulge all your inner secrets, but you should share with your mentees similar experiences to them. This could be as basic as saying that you too were homesick when you came to university or that you were worried about your first assignment. It might be helpful for you to consider why you trust some people but not others: what is different about your interactions with and knowledge about them? Repeated examples of reliability are often associated with trust. If you know someone who is always or often late, you do not trust them to turn up on time. A further useful exercise might be to consider who you would be comfortable sharing your personal concerns with and why.

Trustworthiness is obviously very difficult to teach, with perhaps the options limited to thinking about the possible impact on mentees and connecting this with the mentor's own experiences of relationships. Your peer mentor training will likely look at possible scenarios for this. However, you can develop this attribute for yourself by reflecting on your own experiences, as it is often easier to identify with such aspects if you have personal experience or have been close to it via a close friend or family member. It might also be helpful to talk to past mentors or mentees with stories connected to the characteristic of trustworthiness.

Case scenario: A mentee implies to their mentor that they are attracted to one of the other mentors. The mentor responds by talking casually about this during their session. At the next meeting this mentor mentions what the mentee has said. While they do not give a name it is probably somewhat obvious who the mentee is. The mentees then tend to react slightly differently to this mentee, which is noted by the mentee. As a result the mentee feels awkward and embarrassed and tends to avoid attending future sessions.

The mentee's feedback for the programme notes their dissatisfaction with the programme and comments that they did not get on well with their mentor.

Consider how you would deal with this information and how you might support the mentee to make him feel valued, supported and comfortable attending peer sessions.

Interdependent attitude to mentoring, mentees and programme staff

This characteristic refers to the ability of the mentor to connect, share their own experiences with and learn from the mentees. Engaging in this learning journey with the support of programme staff encapsulates the ideal of a cohesive and con-nected learning community, which is at the heart of what peer mentoring is all about.

Developing this characteristic requires the realisation that we are all on a learn-ing journey and that this occurs more effectively and efficiently as a community. A part of this is recognising that everyone has opinions and that these should be valued. An opinion can never be wrong as the opinion belongs to the individual. You may not agree with their view but it is the way that you deal with these diver-gent opinions that is key. Having mentees with differing opinions can be challeng-ing for a mentor, especially if the topic is emotive. Partly for this reason it can be a good idea to have the mentee group agree a set of ground rules at the beginning of the peer programme. This should include aspects such as 'everyone's opinion will be valued' and 'everyone will show mutual respect for each other'. Regardless of whether there is a set of ground rules in place, such situations require careful mediating. Ensuring that you set the example of respect for others' opinions, giv-ing everyone an equal opportunity to speak, and reminding the mentees of the goals of the peer programme can go a long way towards effectively dealing with such issues. Extremely difficult or aggressive behaviour should be notified to the staff member responsible for the programme.

Your training should help to show you how effective collaborative learning can be and how it operates through group work activities or scenarios. Developing yourself in this area could involve reflecting on your experiences of group learning and study activities. Consider how the interdependent nature of the experience enhanced the learning for all involved, and that the greater the level of engage-ment by all parties, the greater the level of learning achieved.

Mentees generally find that they really appreciate this interdependence once they comprehend the effectiveness and usefulness of how a full positive approach to their engagement with it impacts on themselves. However, you should note that this is not always an easy idea to get across to mentees.

Empathy

Connecting with another person's feelings is an important aspect of peer mentor-ing. Understanding how their situation and experiences have impacted on them emotionally is not just about knowing what they feel; it is also about aligning your own feelings with theirs. This can be very difficult to achieve if you have not experienced the same thing. Trying to put yourself in your mentees' shoes, seeing the situation from their perspective and appreciating the influence of their back-ground will help you develop empathy for them.

To be empathetic is to try to understand your mentees' emotional response to a situation. There may be a number of factors influencing that response which may or may not be directly connected with the situation in question. For example, if someone is depressed or sad due to the loss of a family member, they may have unusual responses to quite normal situations. Hence understanding this response requires an appreciation of the other possible factors which you may or may not be aware of. Trying to ensure you avoid jumping to conclusions about the reasons for another's actions or reactions is therefore an important skill to master. If a mentee's actions or reactions seem unusual for the situation, you may need to try to find out the reason. Doing this in a sensitive and caring manner is part of demonstrating your empathy and will help your mentee overcome, or at least deal with, the situation.

Training for the characteristic of empathy is quite a difficult task for both trainer and trainee. You might find it best to consider possible scenarios, watch and reflect on appropriate TV programmes, and undertake role play with your fellow mentors in order to try to experience different situations that might be encountered by your mentees. Discussing experiences with other mentors, both present and past, might also provide an insight into how to further develop this aspect. Additional guidance might be available from your university health and wellbeing staff, who may also be willing to provide a talk on this area.

> *Case scenario: A mentor in psychology has a group of five mentees. One of these mentees seems quite upset and reports to the mentor that he is feeling very homesick and lonely. The mentor asks him some questions to try to encourage him to talk further about his feelings. He explains where he comes from and about his family life, and that he has never been away from home for more than a day before. He notes he feels lost and as if he has no one to turn to. The mentor listens carefully, paraphrasing what the mentee has said at appropriate points and clarifying the situation. The mentor also shares with the mentee that they too experienced homesickness during the first few weeks. In suggesting that the mentee look at joining a few societies, they encourage them to connect with other students with similar interests. The mentor also offers to meet with the mentee again and suggests a possible day and time.*
>
> The mentee reported that they felt the mentor understood their situation and was able to connect with them with a caring and supportive attitude.
>
> How might you support this mentee? Would you offer different advice or use a different approach?

Personality match with mentee

Personality is of course very individual with no two people exactly alike. Many mentors and mentees find that they can get on with each other quite well, that they have common values and a positive appreciation for each other's culture. However, sometimes there is a clash which can be difficult to overcome without careful pre-planning and training.

Learning how to connect with your mentees from different cultures and backgrounds requires an accepting and broad-minded individual. This can be developed partly through informal non-judgemental information exchange about different cultures, backgrounds and beliefs. To keep this away from personal descriptions it is probably best to start with reading material which might be obtained from your university's departments dealing with international and Erasmus students, or the equality and diversity office. Moving on from this could involve personal stories from previous mentors and mentees. This then is not so much about trying to match personalities but about you as a mentor gaining an appreciation for and acceptance of the variety of people which you might encounter in your role. The range of students will not just encompass students from other countries but also home students whose lives have been different from yours. As mentor you will need to try to accept these differences and help your mentees do the same. As a part of this you need to be sensitive to the needs and situations of your mentees. For example, ensuring you choose appropriate venues to meet where there will be limited financial expenses for your mentees demonstrates sensitivity to those mentees who may struggle financially and be embarrassed about it.

You may develop your appreciation and comprehension of this aspect further by engaging in reflection on your initial impressions of your mentees. Consider what you think they are like as individuals and what types of personality they have. Are they outgoing, brash and overly confident, or are they shy, quiet and reserved? How does this make you feel about them? You may then want to discuss your impressions with your fellow mentors and look for ways to bring your group of mentees together to develop a positive learning environment for all.

Having an appreciation and understanding of personality and the various factors that connect with this is highly valued by not just mentees but also employers, so it is a useful skill to develop. Business managers and leaders often find this an essential skill to enable them to maximise business outcomes, hence the importance attached to this attribute by employers.

Enthusiasm

Enthusiasm in mentors for the mentoring role and its various activities is a vital ingredient much appreciated by mentees. Your role as a mentor is to provide support and encouragement to your mentees to assist them in their studies and university life.

Engaged mentors who appear motivated instil confidence and enthusiasm in their mentees, thereby guiding them on the road to success. You have no doubt encountered really enthusiastic teachers, coaches and trainers whose enthusiasm spreads across a group. Enthusiasm is almost contagious and can help mentees develop interest in a topic. Sports psychologists see enthusiasm and motivation as key factors in sporting success: elite athletes must push themselves to extremes to reach the top, which would be impossible without self-motivation and enthusiasm. Is this merely good goal setting or is it something more than that? As a peer mentor you can set yourself goals but you will need inner enthusiasm to really excel in your role.

Developing your enthusiasm is no easy task. Like empathy, enthusiasm is difficult to teach or learn. We are all enthusiastic about something in our lives, be it a sport, a hobby, a career, etc. However, developing enthusiasm for something you have a limited amount of interest in is very challenging. If you are not highly interested in all aspects of mentoring, this might be a challenge for you. One answer is to find some aspect of mentoring that really interests you and consider what connections there are with the rest of the mentoring role. Seeing the role as a connected whole and realising how the less interesting aspects are key for those areas that really interest you will help develop your enthusiasm for all aspects.

Another avenue to develop enthusiasm is to find fun ways to deliver your mentoring. Generally, enjoyment of an activity enhances enthusiasm, as you have no doubt experienced in other aspects of your life. Locating fun activities might be a somewhat time-consuming but highly beneficial task as you will be able to use them repeatedly with different groups or even the same group with variations. Try brainstorming different ideas with your fellow mentors and ask previous mentors for their suggestions. Often a quite boring topic can be made more interesting by turning the session into a game. You may even find that asking your mentees to think of a way to turn a topic into a game sparks their interest. You will probably find you gain much greater satisfaction from your involvement in your peer programme if you can find these fun ways to develop interest for a topic in your mentees.

Being enthusiastic in your role as a mentor, whether that is mentoring a group or individuals, is plainly obvious to mentees. Enthusiasm does not need to be excessive but should ideally be sufficient to instil confidence and interest in your mentees for the goals of the mentoring programme. Mentees are more likely to participate in the peer programme when you as their mentor display enthusiasm and hence belief in that programme and its goals.

> *Case scenario: A mentor in a history peer programme generally uses texts to support the peer programme sessions. However, they see that mentees become bored and disengaged with this approach. Hence they investigate avenues to bring the topic to life for their mentees. They decide to do a series of activities, recreating the different periods and events with connections to the modern-day situation and thinking that has been covered by the tutors. They get their mentees to devise ways to bring about this recreation through dress, language and actions. They bring in items to assist them in role playing the periods and events leading to discussion around their course themes.*
>
> The mentees feel really engaged and involved in this innovative and active approach. They report increased understanding of the subject and an overall enjoyment of the peer programme. As a result the mentor gains greater satisfaction from the experience and this in turn enhances their own enthusiasm.
>
> How might you enhance engagement with your peer sessions, what changes might you make and what resources would they require?

Flexibility

Being adaptable and flexible in your approach to mentoring aids the development of a good mentor–mentee relationship. This partly comprises acceptance of the differences presented by your mentees. Mentees will come from a wide variety of backgrounds and cultures, and having a flexible, unbiased approach will help them connect with you. Similarly, mentees will present a significant variation in ability, which you will need to accept and accommodate.

Dealing sensitively with this range in ability will require you to devote some time to thinking about and planning your sessions. Preparing a session to support those of a lesser ability while also providing activities for the more able is a challenge. It can often be a good idea to draw on those with more knowledge and understanding to assist the other members of the group. However, you will need to arrange this so that your less able mentees do not feel ignorant or less valued.

Another aspect of flexibility is in your willingness to accept and incorporate useful suggestions by your mentees. If your mentees feel that you listen to and take note of what they say, they are more likely to develop a good connection with you. A further activity here of discussing the suggestions with the group demonstrates interest in their ideas and hence them. This simultaneously tends to enhance their respect for you as their mentor.

Training for flexibility development will obviously involve a variety of activities. This might include learning about different cultures through texts and discussion, gaining an appreciation of ability levels via talks with academic staff, and setting realistic goals for yourself and your mentees. Setting these realistic targets can involve discussion within the mentee group about how to accommodate the variation in ability levels using a varied step approach, where all can work to their own level.

Having flexibility in your approach to mentoring will be much appreciated by your mentees as they will all feel valued, accommodated and accepted within the group.

Case scenario: A first-year peer group in engineering comprises students with a range of academic topic backgrounds. Some have gained high-level qualifications in maths while others have not. The peer mentor considers how to accommodate this variation in ability. They devise with their tutor a set of worksheets for the mentees to undertake during the peer sessions. The early problems on the worksheets address the more basic concepts and then the problems progress in difficulty, building on these basic concepts. The mentor offers guidance to mentees as necessary, helping both those with less experience and those with higher ability levels to progress at their own pace and level.

The mentees feel appropriately supported and accommodated, and the mentor is able to fulfil their role effectively.

In what way would you add flexibility to your peer sessions to accommodate differences in ability in your mentee group?

Activity 4.5

Read through the case scenarios given above. Consider your reactions to these and think about how you might deal with these situations. You might also wish to discuss the scenarios with your fellow mentors.

Training for successful mentoring

You should receive some comprehensive initial training to ensure that you are fully prepared for the complex role you have taken on. The approach to training should address all facets of the role and may take up to two days to fully explore all aspects. As part of this training, some time should be given to exploring and supporting the development of the core psychosocial aspects as addressed above. In addition to this initial training you will find it useful to continue your own development through reading, reflection and attending other developmental activities which might be delivered by your institution. The characteristics needed to be a good mentor are also key attributes which will make you successful in all aspects of your life from personal relationships to professional achievements. These vital skills are highly valued by employers, community groups and international organisations and are thus well worth the time and effort needed to hone them.

Conclusion

This chapter has considered the characteristics of effective peer mentors. The highly varied nature of your role as a peer mentor requires an array of attributes, including the psychosocial and career characteristics identified in Terrion and Leonard's (2007) review. These characteristics, such as empathy and trustworthiness, are often thought to be unchangeable, but we suggest that you can develop these if you are sufficiently willing and enthusiastic. Your peer mentor training should attend to these characteristics, but this is no easy task; it requires an innovative approach involving activities such as role play, scenarios and personal experience talks. When you have gained a good level of these characteristics you will be a highly effective peer mentor and will be well prepared for your future interactions within a professional work setting.

Key points from this chapter

- Effective peer mentors require a range of characteristics.
- All characteristics can be developed to some extent.
- Developing psychosocial characteristics requires willingness and enthusiasm.

5

Academic Support

By the end of this chapter you will:

- have an understanding of some of the theoretical basis for providing academic support
- have an overview of what happens in a typical mentoring session
- have a range of case studies to consider and compare with your own mentoring experience
- have an introduction to some basic teaching techniques which mentors can employ in sessions.

This chapter is all about the academic support part of being a mentor. In many ways this is the aspect of the role which attracts mentors the most, but it is also the most difficult element of being a mentor. The chapter introduces you to the ways in which people learn, such as different learning styles; the contexts in which learning can be applied; the way in which mentoring can create a community of learning; and how mentoring can help to support and scaffold learning. It then moves to some case studies which illustrate examples of what mentors have encountered while providing academic support. Finally, there is a more practical description of a typical mentoring session and examples of some of the techniques which mentors can use to engage mentees.

Why do mentors provide academic support?

Although, as has been established earlier in this book, there are many different types of mentoring within higher education institutions, one thing that is usually present within a student mentoring relationship is a focus on academic or study support. The rationale for involving student mentors in academic support is that, although you are not yet expert in your subject, you have some recent experience of learning the topics and modules which newer students will be encountering for the first time and therefore you can offer the benefit of this experience. Some mentor schemes select mentors on the basis of academic success, but it is not necessarily a pre-requisite. In fact, the more common requirement is that mentors are motivated to help others through some of the more bewildering aspects of higher education. Having said that, as a mentor you can play a very valuable role in bridging the gap between student and lecturer, and, because of your recent experience of study, you will also be in a good position to explain difficult concepts and empathise with students who are perhaps finding the pace in class too fast.

What kind of academic support do mentors provide?

It is not intended that mentoring should replace any form of interaction between staff and students; instead it provides additional opportunities for students to interact with each other within collaborative study groups. Mentoring is often attached to specific modules which are deemed difficult by most students so it provides a 'safe environment' for students to discuss ideas, share problems and resolve questions. Mentoring sessions are intended to promote collaborative learning through discussion. They are also a chance for mentors to share experiences. The discussions that you have are usually based on the course materials provided by the tutor (normally via a virtual learning environment (VLE)) or on reading recommended by the tutor. As a mentor you are not expected to introduce new material or re-teach lectures; instead, the emphasis is on encouraging students to compare notes, clarify reading and question ideas that have been introduced in the module. This approach is aimed at consolidating knowledge and gaining confidence in study strategies. Your sessions should be structured to ensure a productive learning environment, but it is anticipated that there will also be an element of informality and fun.

How do mentors support mentees' learning?

The approach to academic support that most university mentor schemes take is based on Vygostsky's (1978) hypothesis that learning is 'socially constructed'. This means that learning takes place in a social context: through discussion and meaning making, whereby a learner takes on new information by fitting it into what they already know. This approach also places emphasis on 'situated learning', which means that new information must be situated in an authentic or relevant context that is, it should be applied to real situations or experiences. As a peer mentor you have a close experience to that of the student(s) you are supporting, which means that you are well placed to help in the construction and assimilation of new knowledge and understanding. You may also be able to relate to the experiences of your mentees so that you can help them to see the new knowledge that they are learning in a context which is relevant to them.

How do mentors help students to develop a sense of belonging at university?

Universities can be understood as communities which have layers of membership. New students are on the outer periphery of the membership, but as they progress through their programme of study they start to penetrate deeper into the university community. This process of belonging is often helped by mentoring programmes whereby a mentor can help to explain and induct newer students into the community. According to Wenger (1998, p73) this is done through three activities: working together (joint enterprise); sharing an understanding of the course content (shared repertoire); and working together as mentor and mentee (mutual engagement). The mentor's role in helping new students to feel a sense of belonging to the learning community is therefore of great importance and something which has long been accepted as an essential element in retaining students in higher education.

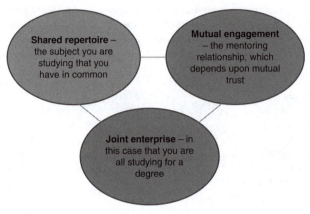

Communities of learning

Adapted from Wenger (1998, p73)

What do mentors do within the learning process?

A mentor's role has various descriptions, one of which is 'facilitator', the focus here being on the mentor enabling their mentee(s) to learn through their own endeavour and experience rather than doing things for them. You may also have encountered the term 'scaffolding' to describe an approach to supporting learning. This term was used by Brown, Collins and Duguid (1989, p39) and in a mentoring context means that the mentor provides a framework which supports learning. This scaffolding is put in place for learners until they are ready to work without it. These descriptions of how mentors support learning are useful starting points. As a mentor you are likely to be involved in all or some of the following:

- supporting the learning experience
- assisting with transition into and within higher education
- enabling enhanced interaction with peers
- providing opportunities for students to become more engaged with their courses
- improving academic achievement
- providing an additional mechanism for feedback and communication between staff and students.

What happens in a typical peer mentoring session?

Peer mentors are typically expected to meet with their mentees once a week for peer support. Sessions are generally scheduled to last just under an hour and groups are usually small or one to one. It is often very difficult to get a teaching room allocated for mentoring sessions and it is not normally appropriate because mentoring groups are small and informal. Often the best spaces for mentoring to take place are discussion zones within libraries, or university cafes. Within the session, although mentors are expected to have a plan, which may be based on weekly lecture topics or may be based on aspects of study skills, it is usually the mentees who set the agenda with the mentor responding to the mentees' needs rather than having a rigid set of topics to follow.

- **Review progress and get feedback:** Mentors have usually done the same or similar modules as their mentees and they are normally given online access to the module(s) to which the mentoring activity is attached, so weekly mentor meetings can follow the lecture topics and mentors often start by asking mentees to say what they have understood from the week's instruction.
- **Checklist of generic study skills:** As well as following the module outline, mentees often have difficulty responding to assessment requirements so it is useful to draw up a checklist of study skills topics which you know will be useful in the module, such as reading, note taking, referencing and essay writing, and focusing on one topic per week.
- **Agree actions:** It might be that, during the course of your review, questions arise that you and the group cannot answer. Therefore it will be necessary for you and your mentees to agree actions such as to ask the tutor a question, or to research a particular concept further. It is best if you can divide the tasks between the members of the group and agree how to share answers, whether online or at the next meeting.
- **Keep a record and share with absent mentees:** If you have taken notes during the review it is useful to share these with all your mentees. This can now be done very easily by taking a picture on your phone of any notes made and sharing it with the group.
- **Closing the session:** It is always reassuring for members of a group to have a formal closing. This can be done in the last five minutes of the session by summarising the main points and perhaps agreeing on a topic for next week.

Common topics on which mentors provide academic support

The academic support which mentors provide usually falls within three broad areas:

- **Study skills**, including topics such as how to write a good report, why referencing is important, how to find reading resources for your subject and what tutors expect from a presentation.
- **Subject-specific content** which mentors have usually encountered the year before.
- **Technical support** with VLEs, online portfolios and text-matching software.

This part of the chapter looks at three areas of study skills and technical support which mentors provide (academic writing, time management and IT support), and it gives examples within discipline contexts of how mentors have helped and the benefits to mentees.

Academic writing

Many students struggle at first with the writing expectations at university. This may be because they have come from a non-traditional route into university, gaining qualifications other than A levels, or they may have had more emphasis on the practical elements of their subject, especially in subjects such as art, music and sports. They may have had a long break from academic work or be from a non-English-speaking background. Although it may be tempting to proofread for your mentee, this goes against the principles of mentoring and is likely to lead to a situation where your mentee feels dependent upon you to check all of their written work before they submit it, which will become very onerous for you and does not instil the independent learning skills which higher education espouses. It might be better to offer to read just one page of a mentee's work, then work together on the writing style and any grammar and spelling issues that you can identify. Or it might be useful to look at model answers together and point out good writing style. (Academic staff are usually happy to provide one or two model answers for students to look at.) It is important to note here that writing style, grammar and spelling can sometimes be highly charged emotional issues for students. Some students may feel very embarrassed by their mistakes, so it is always important to check with your mentee first about what kind of feedback they want on their writing. If you do give feedback on writing, try to ensure a non-judgemental stance about errors because they may be due to dyslexia, second language acquisition, gaps in your mentee's educational experience or something else which you are not aware of. You may feel that your mentee requires more specialist help so you can play an important role in signposting them either to a dyslexia tutor or to a study skills tutor.

Example in a school of pharmacy

In the first year, academic writing for pharmacy students consists of writing lab reports. Many new students worry about what is expected from them with this type of writing, so this is a topic which arises frequently in mentor meetings. The types of help that pharmacy mentors have been able to give are to share notes with their mentees and to explain what is required from them for a lab report. However, some pharmacy mentors have been asked by their mentees to read their report and tell them if it's good. Mentors report being uncomfortable with this request as they do not feel equipped to make a judgement on other students' work and from the mentor training they also know that this is not something which they are supposed to do. However, mentors say that talking about lab reports and sharing knowledge about the requirements helped them to revise the topic themselves and gain confidence in their own writing skills. They also say that their support for mentees' lab reports helped alleviate mentees' anxiety and gave them a reason to engage with mentoring.

Time management

Time management is a major concern for many new university students. This is because it is often their first time away from home, managing their finances, doing all of their own chores, possibly working part-time and building a new social network. Balancing these demands with the course requirements can be a significant challenge for many students. Students who have been within a school system are also often not used to the notion of independent learning because schools provide a lot of support and structure which universities do not. Therefore it can be very challenging for many students to take responsibility for their learning, which involves tasks such as selecting and prioritising reading, cataloguing notes, downloading information and planning assignments. Helpful things that mentors can do with mentees are to look together at modules and assignments to identify deadlines then plot them onto a wall calendar so that they can be easily viewed. It is also then useful to encourage mentees to work backwards from their deadlines to plot realistic interim deadlines for aspects of each task. For example:

Wednesday 23 March	Thursday 24 March	Friday 25 March
• Read books and articles from reading list for essay 1 • Make notes and keep references	• Plan essay in detail • Include what will go into each paragraph	• Draft essay • Read it through and make edits

Example in an arts school

For students on arts and humanities programmes it is common to have very few contact hours – that is, lectures and seminars. Typically, students' timetables may only show six to eight hours of contact time. To a new student this often seems as if they have very little work to do; however, every full-time programme of study is estimated to be the equivalent of 35 to 40 hours taught and self-directed learning per week. This makes time management for arts and humanities students even more important than for students on programmes with more structured lectures and seminars. Mentors in arts-based subjects report that time management is a topic which often occurs in the early stages of their mentoring relationship. Mentors advise on how to structure a typical day, encourage mentees to use the university's facilities, such as studios, rather than work at home, build networks with other students across the years and avoid too much time studying alone, which can lead to issues of isolation and alienation. The support which mentors provide in these areas includes plotting deadlines, insight into how assignment deadlines bunch, and how to book studio space and work with others in groups.

IT skills

Although students are often referred to as 'digital natives', that is people who have grown up with technology and are thought to be IT savvy there are in fact many students (mature and young) who are not very confident when using technology which is new to them. Some of the common issues which mentors report mentees having are with syncing their emails so that they can read all university emails (there is an increasing issue of email blindness as students get bombarded with hundreds of emails a week, with some students going as far as to regard all university emails as spam). There are also issues which can arise from students reading information designed for a PC screen (e.g. timetables) on a phone screen. This often means that they cannot read along a line fluently and have difficulty matching a time with an event because of the screen width. Finally, not all students have access to good computers in top working condition. In many cases, students have used their computer to download a lot of audio visual material and this often results in the computer crashing or processing very slowly. Useful advice which mentors can provide in these situations is to recommend that mentees use the computing facilities on campus. You might also recommend that mentees 'clean' their computer of all the downloads that they no longer need or take it to a shop to get it serviced, (some university IT departments provide this facility).

Example in a school of music

This example of mentors helping mentees to get to grips with IT comes from a music school, but there are many students from a wide variety of schools who are confronted with new technology when they get to university, so it is an area where mentors can provide targeted and useful support. One piece of unfamiliar software which many universities use is online portfolios. These are especially useful tools on programmes where a student may want to record and reflect upon their development. In this example, peer mentors were asked to run an introductory session on how to use an e-portfolio and then provide a time-tabled drop-in for students who wanted further support. In addition to this, mentors offered advice via email to students working on their portfolios from home. Mentees reported that they found the advice from their fellow students very easy to follow and that they appreciated the 'in-time' nature of the online and drop-in support they received. For mentors the e-portfolio workshops provided them with a good hands-on opportunity to be useful to new students and a good way to review their own use of the software.

Activity 5.1

What is your experience of supporting another student's learning? Write a short case study about a generic study skill or use of technology where you have supported another student to learn. How did you help them to learn and what did you gain from the experience?

Teaching techniques

Although mentors are not teachers, many of the techniques you use within the mentoring relationship are teaching techniques. Overall, the role of being a mentor will enhance your communication skills and equip you better for graduate employment. In fact, many mentors go on to think about teaching, training or coaching as a career after they graduate. The following section introduces you to some teaching techniques which are very useful for mentors.

Ice-breakers: It is very important to get the right tone within mentoring sessions so you will need to get to know your mentees quickly. Therefore it is vital to learn your mentees' names and be able to recognise them around campus. It is also useful to know something about them and find common areas of interest. Ice-breaker games are a good way to start getting to know your mentees, but be careful not to overuse them. There are plenty of examples of Ice-breakers which you can look up on the internet. Here are just a few tried and tested ones:

- **Find three things in common:** This is a nice way to get to know one or two people. First, get mentees to talk together to identify three things which they have in common. It is good to encourage them to go beyond the obvious – for example, we are both studying the same subject or we both live in halls – to think about which countries they have visited, what pets they have or what films/books/music they love. Once they have found three things in common, get them to feed this back to you and the whole group.
- **Name association animals:** It is really important that you remember the names of your mentees. This ice breaker is a fun way to do this. Ask mentees to say their name and then think of an animal which starts with the same first letter, such as Louise – lion, Abdul – armadillo, Chi – chicken, Sid – snake. This can result in some fun and it helps you to remember who is who.
- **Human bingo:** This ice breaker is designed for a large group. First, design a grid with lots of questions within it (see the example below). Students must mingle with each other to find one person who can respond positively to each question and then write that person's name in the appropriate square. When they have done that they shout bingo!

Has been to Paris	Has tried yoga	Has been to university before	Has never broken any bones
Can speak a foreign language	Doesn't like chocolate	Has been stung by a bee	Owns a car
Has been to India	Has a pet cat	Has more than one middle name	Doesn't have a Facebook page
Doesn't like shopping	Has children	Can play a musical instrument	Is wearing something green

4. **Truth or lie:** This ice breaker is better to do when mentees know each other and you reasonably well. The idea is to say two things about yourself which are true and one thing which is false, and for the listeners to correctly identify the false information.

Group work techniques

Group review: A very useful exercise is to review a topic by writing down all students' contributions and then working as a group to expand and extend their learning by adding examples and building knowledge together. This helps students to 'situate' their learning in a context they can relate to.

Group discussion: This is probably the most common activity associated with collaborative learning. However, it is not always easy to get a good discussion going. It may be necessary to ask mentees to do something first, such as read a short text, look through notes or watch a video clip, then identify the main points and discuss.

Cluster discussions: This technique is useful for bigger groups. A cluster group should consist of no more than three people. It is often useful to do this if the topic you are discussing is complex and therefore you need clusters to discuss different questions within the topic and then feed back.

Mind mapping: Mind maps (Buzan, 2002) use research on how the brain works to retain and store information, such as making connections, using colour and images. The visual and connected nature of a mind map enables students to make links between ideas and remember how ideas are connected. Mentors can introduce mentees to the concept of mind mapping and spend time working on mind maps together.

Graphic recording: Graphic recording (Dosad, 2015) is perhaps just a formal way of describing doodling for academic purposes. The idea behind this is that images can convey meaning and show understanding. This can be particularly useful for students building their academic glossary so that they not only remember the new item of vocabulary but also understand the meaning of the word. Mentors do not need to be artistic to be good at graphic recording as it is a communication tool rather than an art skill.

Question techniques: Asking questions is a skill in itself. Sometimes questions meet silence and other times the room erupts into lively debate. It is useful as a mentor to spend time before the session thinking of good questions which will provoke discussion. You may want to write these down so that your mentees can see that you have prepared and they can respond to complex questions by re-reading them during the discussion. As you probably already know, questions can be of varying degrees of difficulty. You may be familiar with terms such as 'open' and 'closed' questions – that is those which require a single answer and those which can be answered in a number of different ways. Questions can be categorised further using Bloom's taxonomy of educational objectives (1956).

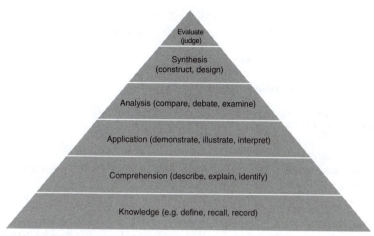

Question Techniques pyramid
Adapted from Bloom et al. (1956)

By looking at the verbs in a question you can ascertain what level of question you are asking. When you are planning a session for your mentees, try to make sure that you ask questions in a staged way so that they move from recall questions through to evaluation. For example, you may have a topic about methods of social research which could be structured through staged questions to mentees such as:

- What methods of social research are there?
- Describe what an online questionnaire is.
- In what situations would an online questionnaire be useful?
- What are the strengths and weaknesses of an online questionnaire?
- Why might you use an online questionnaire rather than a spoken interview?
- Design your own online questionnaire to find out about ....
- Having read about different methods of social research, evaluate a recent study on a topic of your interest.

Staged questions such as those above will help your mentees to build confidence early on and enable you to check their knowledge before moving on to more difficult questions which require critical thinking.

Redirecting questions: As a mentor your role is not to know the answer to every question. In fact, it is much better if you do not answer questions directly but try to redirect questions to enable mentees to think about things. For example, if you are asked what is meant by the term 'post-modernism', or why 'world music' is a contested term, or how 'non-traditional families' are affected by social policy, it might be useful to reserve your answer until you have redirected it back to your mentees. Here are some ways to do this:

- What do other people think?
- Has that been covered in class?

- Can you remember what was said in the lecture about that?
- What have you read about that?
- Is there anything else?
- Can you think of a current example?
- Can you make links between x and y?
- Can you see any issues, difficulties or contradictions in this?

Activity 5.2

Think of a topic you could do with mentees in your subject. Write some questions for students using Bloom's Taxonomy (see question technique pyramid) to make the questions harder as the mentees progress through them.

Pair work: Working in pairs is a fast and effective way to involve everyone in discussion. It is especially useful if you want students to discuss something quickly and then bring their attention back to the whole group again.

Quick quiz: Students generally like the idea of a quiz on a topic. It can be useful to do this as a team-based activity so it does not feel like a test and so that mentees are encouraged to discuss their answers with each other. You may want to team up with another mentor's group to do this to make it more fun and get more people involved. Once you have done one quick quiz you could ask mentees to think of quiz questions about another topic to test each other on.

Organising information on topics: Students often feel overwhelmed by the volume of information they get within a module. Therefore another useful mentoring activity is to use the session to organise what they have learned and make a bullet point handout or poster.

Revision sessions: One element of mentoring sessions which is always popular with mentees is sessions aimed at revision for exams. There are lots of activities you can do to help students to plan and organise their revision, be more effective in their revision and perform their best in exams.

Activity 5.3

Think of a topic within your subject which you have already encountered and which you are confident about. Make a poster using a spider diagram, mind map or visual images to display all the information that you think mentees need to know on this topic.

Planning revision: It is very helpful to spend at least one mentoring session getting mentees to plot their exams on a planner and then divide their revision time evenly between the exams they have.

Effective revision: Some of the things you can do within a mentoring session are:

- Look at past papers and discuss questions, or tackle one question under timed conditions and then share the answers for discussion.

- Create topic posters with all the information about a topic in words and images on one poster.

Exam strategies: Exams are often a cause of high anxiety for students, so it is useful to reserve one of your mentoring sessions to talk about what to do within an exam. Issues which are useful to cover include what to do if your mind goes blank, a quick relaxation exercise (see the breathing exercise below) and reminders about doing the easier questions first in order to warm up to the exam.

Activity 5.4

Breathing relaxation technique

To help your mentees you can teach them a breathing relaxation technique to use during exams. Ask mentees to sit in a balanced and relaxed posture then take one deep breath with their mouth open and slowly release it, imagining their breath exiting their mouth. Tell mentees to repeat this three to five times before bringing their focus back to the exam.

Gathering feedback: This is a vital facilitating skill that can quite often be rushed. If you have given groups a discussion question, it is essential that you provide time for them to feed back their answer to you and the whole group. In order for this to happen in a structured way you may find that asking a member of the group to scribe their group's discussion is useful.

Meeting resistance: Although mentoring is an informal and voluntary activity, students can behave confrontationally or disinterestedly in groups. This can present mentors with considerable challenge, but hopefully it will be something that you will be able to overcome. You have some key factors on your side: first, you are one of them, so you have no need to exert authority; second, you are not responsible for their grades – they are; and, finally, if all else fails and you feel that one of your mentees is not mature enough to respond well to this style of learning support, you can ask him or her to leave. In addition there are some things to bear in mind which will help strengthen your role as a mentor. For example:

- Ensure that you are prepared for sessions, but also try to be flexible and respond to questions.
- If you see mentees around campus, try to invite them personally to your sessions.
- Try to use the language of the discipline and encourage mentees to build a glossary of terms.
- If you ask questions that require thinking time, try to relax and allow a short wait time for responses.
- Try to avoid interrupting mentees when they are talking.
- Refer to the module regularly and check that students are aware of requirements and deadlines.
- Make sure your mentoring is helpful, but try not to create dependency.

Activity 5.5

What do you think you should do in the following two common scenarios?

A student asks if you can read their essay for mistakes before they submit it the next day. Although you feel that you would like to help, you are a little uncomfortable with this request, partly because you are not a grammar expert and partly because as it is the day before you feel that there is not really time to teach your mentee anything. What might you say and how might you re-set boundaries?

A student does not participate in conversation during a mentoring session. You have noticed that the student is shy anyway, but you know that if she can speak up in a mentoring session this will help her to develop confidence for seminar participation. You have felt unconfident in the past so you want to share with her some of the techniques you have used to overcome this feeling. What advice would you give her?

Reviewing your academic support as a mentor

Within any professional role it is necessary to review your practice in order to evaluate your strengths and weaknesses, and to identify gaps in your skills and knowledge that will lead you to make continuous improvements to your work as a mentor. This is a good habit to get into as a mentor. The following questions can be used as a starting point for you to review the academic support you provide as a mentor.

Activity 5.6

What elements of the academic support that I provide are going well?

What do I find difficult about providing academic support to mentees?

How do other people (mentors, lecturers, teachers in the past, coaches, etc.) do this better?

What could I do differently?

What small steps can I put in place to ensure change and development?

Conclusion

This chapter has highlighted that the main reasons for engaging mentors in the higher education relationship between staff and students are because there is often a gap between what lecturers expect and what students understand, and because mentors have recent experience of study. Therefore mentors provide a vital bridge and help with transition into and within university. The theory that underpins the academic support within a mentoring relationship is based on notions of collaborative learning, situated learning and communities of learning, as well as facilitation, participation and support. When this role is fully understood by mentors, they can provide invaluable support to mentees' studies. This can lead to improved grades and increased academic confidence for mentees, and it has the added benefit for mentors' academic performance of revising their knowledge and communicating ideas.

Key points from this chapter

- Academic support for mentoring is underpinned by education theory on situated learning, communities of learning and student-centred learning.
- The techniques that mentors use for providing academic support include questioning, facilitation, support and creating visual materials.
- There are many generic academic support topics which mentors from a wide variety of disciplines will encounter.

Chapter

6

Social Support

By the end of this chapter you will:

- be clear about the boundaries of your role as a mentor in the context of social and personal issues
- have an understanding of the skills involved in active listening
- be aware of the importance of signposting mentees to the correct professional support
- reflect on your own emotional intelligence
- use case studies to think about how you might respond to real social issues which mentors encounter.

Most peer mentoring schemes in higher education have an explicit focus on academic support for mentees. However, because of the nature of developing a close and often one-to-one relationship, there are implicit social or wellbeing elements to mentoring relationships. The social support which mentors provide is different from what is offered by professional support services on campus because as a mentor you represent 'living proof' that you have survived the course so far. In this way you can offer an 'authentic voice' from a student perspective and give practical support on issues such as homesickness, managing competing demands, and planning and organisation. New students often report a sense of feeling overwhelmed in the first few months of being a student so the aim of mentors' social support is to help your mentees to persist in higher education and to believe in themselves. This can potentially lead you into situations which are deeper and more complex than you may be able or willing to handle. This is why much of the generic training for mentors at universities focuses on establishing an honest and trusting relationship but at the same time having an awareness of your limitations and establishing firm boundaries.

A diverse student population can present challenges for mentoring relationships. There may be some peer mentoring schemes where students are matched according to gender to address key issues which the university considers to be important; for example, female students may be matched in science, technology, engineering and maths subjects, or male students may be matched to improve attendance or motivation. There may also be mentoring schemes which target students from black and ethnic minority backgrounds (BME) to encourage greater participation and to address the attainment gap between BME and white students. The social support needed for these targeted mentoring schemes may require specialist training, which this chapter does not offer. Instead, it gives general strategies for establishing and maintaining strong boundaries. It also outlines the importance of interpersonal skills and considers whether these can be learned. There are also practical exercises for you to use with your mentees to help you discuss issues and offer support to resolve them.

Activity 6.1

Support services

Do you know what support services are available at your institution? If you do, can you provide a fairly detailed explanation of the sorts of aspects of students' lives they can help with? Also, can you explain what that support entails?

Ideally, this is the sort of information it would be helpful for you to find out, preferably by talking to that department. In so doing you can ascertain when they feel you should direct mentees to them. They may also provide you with some information leaflets that you can refer to during your sessions with mentees.

Mentoring behaviours

The mentor's role in social and welfare support has various descriptions. It may be helpful for you to bear in mind the mentoring behaviours identified by Klasen & Clutterbuck (2001) which are divided into those you should always, sometimes and never use.

- **Always:** Listen with empathy; share experience; form a mutual learning friendship; develop insight through reflection; be a sounding board; and encourage.
- **Sometimes:** Use coaching behaviours; use counselling behaviours; challenge assumptions; and be a role model.
- **Never:** Discipline, judge or formally appraise.

This guidance is helpful because in your mentoring role you play an important function, but there are also limitations which should be borne in mind.

What kind of social support might mentors provide?

The social support which mentors provide varies significantly. This is particularly due to the increasingly diverse nature of student populations. Many reports suggest that student wellbeing issues seem to be becoming more and more common as students are under more pressure due to high fees; the need to do paid work alongside their studies; external and internal pressure to get a 'good degree'

(1st or 2:1); lack of graduate employment; and the range of diverse educational backgrounds that students come from. The following examples aim to enable you to reflect on how you might respond to these issues if you were confronted with them. It will also give you an opportunity to reflect on the skills and attributes that you may develop as a result of these challenges.

Time management

Two of the initial problems that new students face are establishing a work–life balance at university and becoming an independent learner. These aspects of student life are often challenging because, for many students, university is the first time that they have lived away from home, managed their own money and not been supervised by teachers or parents to do regular homework. Therefore some of your mentoring support can be channelled towards helping your mentees with work–life balance and independent learning.

One strategy which you may find useful to use with your mentees is to ask them to complete a life wheel diagram. You can copy the one below, or do your own with different headings in the segments. Ask your mentees to put a dot on each dissecting line to show how satisfied they are with each aspect of their life. Dots near to the centre indicate that they are not very satisfied and those towards the edge of the circle indicate satisfaction. Ideally students' circles will be relatively balanced. If the wheel is not well balanced you can help your mentees to think through how they might be able to achieve more balance in their lives.

Life wheel

It is very useful to keep copies of the life wheel and then repeat the exercise at regular intervals. By looking through all of their 'wheels' your mentees can get a good impression of when their life feels out of balance. It might be that self-study scores low. If this is the case it can be useful to ask your mentees to list the activities which they think make up self-study, such as reading, library searching, internet searching, rewriting notes, listening to lectures online and talking with other students about assignments. By doing this, mentees can see what they spend their time on and also perhaps identify self-study activities that they don't do and therefore could build into their lives. The life wheel can also be a helpful way for you to help your mentees think about the goals they want to set themselves. For example, if their score for self-study is low, they may then think of all the different self-study they do and focus on increasing this by half an hour for each activity.

Goal setting and action planning

Once your mentees have done a life wheel and identified an area to work on, this can become a goal. However, goals are often not easy to achieve (otherwise they would already be done), so it's important to make an action plan to achieve the goal. Action planning is often broken down using SMART objectives which help to identify the steps needed to achieve a goal. You can ask your mentees to do their own SMART action plans for an aspect of their lives they want to improve.

Goal: To do more self-study	
Specific	Clearly define your goal, such as *Read one chapter or one article every weekday.*
Measurable	Set a goal which you can measure, such as *Keep a record of the chapters and articles that you read with very brief notes about them.*
Achievable	Set goals which are within your capability and try not to make them too ambitious because this is likely to result in failure, such as *Improve my marks by 5%.*
Relevant	Make sure that the tasks within your action plan build towards your goal, such as *Read for an hour each day.*
Time bound	Set a timescale for your goal, such as *Keep a reading record for one term and then review it.*

Decision making

Another aspect of independent life which often comes to students for the first time when they are at university is having to make decisions which affect their life. Many people at any age struggle with this and find it quite hard to make a confident decision about what they should do. As a mentor your role is to support your mentees in making decisions. You should not feel that you have to advise or influence your mentees; the decisions need to be their own. One way to do this is simply to encourage them to make a list of the options they have and then write the pros and cons. This might be about decisions such as where to live in year two, whether to do a year in industry or which module options to take.

	Pros	Cons
Living in halls	Good Wi-Fi connection All bills included Close to uni	Noisy Can't choose who I share with Unlikely to get a room
Living in a private house	Can choose who to live with Cheaper rent than halls Can share cooking/shopping with friends	Bills on top Might be difficult to share with friends Landlord might be difficult

Another widely used tool to help make decisions is the SWOT (strengths, weaknesses, opportunities and threats) analysis. You can use this with your mentees to help them identify what their strengths and weaknesses are and then to predict what might be an opportunity or a threat on the horizon. It is a useful tool to ask your mentees to do and then to discuss together. The discussion should enable your mentees to further develop their SWOT diagrams and prioritise activities.

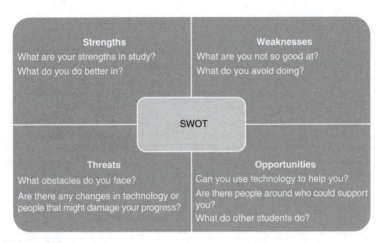

SWOT analysis

Developing interpersonal skills

Although there is a belief among some that interpersonal skills are something you either have or haven't got, there are of course ways in which you can develop this aspect of yourself in order to help and support others. One of the ways in which this can be done is through reflecting on your interactions with others. This is done by identifying key incidents in your interactions, recording your feelings about each situation, analysing what went well or not so well, considering the reasons behind this and then making a plan for the next time you encounter a similar situation.

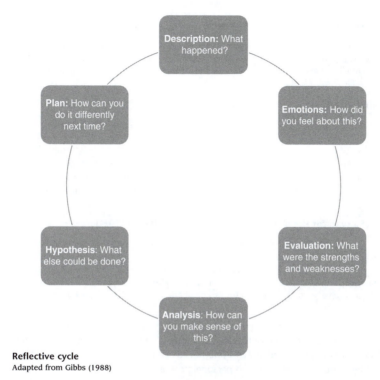

Reflective cycle
Adapted from Gibbs (1988)

The example below of a reflective journal entry shows the reflective process as a way of understanding human interaction. The stages of reflection enable you to understand the situation better and to think about how you might approach a similar situation in the future. In many mentoring programmes, mentors are encouraged or required to keep a reflective journal of their mentoring experience to help process difficult issues which may arise. This is explored further in Chapter 9.

Reflective journal entry

Identify key incidents in your interactions with others

Today I met with my mentee. She has been feeling low because she is homesick and she misses her dog.

Record your feelings about the situation

I felt quite sorry for her at first because I remember what it was like for me starting university in a strange country, not understanding the local accent and not having any friends. However, I began to feel a bit resentful of her because she is not an international student and in fact her home is only two hours away by train so she can easily visit home if she needs to. I also thought she was being a bit weird about her dog. I think some of my lack of empathy came across to her and I feel bad about that.

Analyse what went well or not so well

Although it was good that she felt she could tell me about feeling homesick and I could share with her some of my feelings about being far from home, our very different life experiences meant that we soon realised our differences rather than our similarities.

Consider the reasons behind this

I think that because I am an international student and she is a home student we have different perceptions of what it means to be far from home. I felt a bit impatient with her that she was feeling homesick when from my point of view she is still at home. But as I have pondered this, I realise that it's not just about distance, it's also about change. I think I could have helped her to see this change in a more positive way rather than comparing her distance with mine and making her feel that she was making a fuss about nothing.

Make a plan for the next time you encounter a similar situation

I have decided to share with her some of the things I did to help me settle in at university. I will encourage her to see the positive aspects of life at university and help her to identify a club or society which might help her make new friends and connections. I will also try to be more enthusiastic about seeing pictures of her dog and encourage her to display a picture somewhere.

Although, as has been mentioned before, mentors are not counsellors, there are some counselling behaviours which can be useful in a mentoring role. Non-directive counselling put forward initially by Rogers (1951) emphasises three core conditions which help support someone with personal problems.

- **An accepting stance:** This means that you accept what the mentee is telling you without judgement or conditions.
- **Sensitivity:** This means that you try to show through empathy and understanding that you are supportive of the mentee. You try to imagine how your mentee feels by identifying a similar feeling that you have experienced.
- **Genuineness:** This relates to openness to expressing your own feelings, but in a value-free way which ensures that you do not sound like you are making judgements about your mentee or their actions.

Activity 6.2

Try to identify a time when your interactions with another person who you were trying to support did not go well. Write out a reflective journal entry as above and then use Rogers' core conditions to help you think through how you might do things differently if you find yourself in a similar situation.

Developing emotional intelligence

Emotional intelligence is 'the ability to monitor one's own and others' feelings and emotions, to discriminate among them and to use this information to guide one's thinking' (Mayer and Salovey, 1993). It is now becoming highly sought after by employers who recognise that these qualities are an asset to their organisations. Experience as a mentor should enable you to give concrete examples of how you have used your emotional intelligence to help others. Mayer and Salovey (1993) identify four branches of emotional intelligence. The table below demonstrates the way in which emotional intelligence is crucial to being a successful and effective mentor. As you read it, consider to what extent you are able to meet these traits and where you think you might need further training.

Branches of emotional intelligence	Definition	Application to mentoring
Perceiving emotions	The ability to perceive emotions in oneself and others as well as in objects, art, stories, music and other stimuli.	It will be useful for you to be able to perceive when your mentee is experiencing difficult emotions and also reflect on when you have been challenged emotionally.
Facilitating thought	The ability to generate, use and feel emotion as necessary to communicate feelings or employ them in other cognitive processes.	You might need to talk with your mentee about the emotions they are experiencing.
Understanding emotions	The ability to understand emotional information, to understand how emotions combine and progress through relationship transitions, and to appreciate such emotional meanings.	Your relationship with your mentee will last for a term or a year so you will need to recognise that their emotions towards a situation may change over time.
Managing emotions	The ability to be open to feelings, and to modulate them in oneself and others so as to promote personal understanding and growth.	This may be something that you can do through humour or conversation which shows your support but doesn't encourage the mentee to ruminate on negative emotions.

Knowing your boundaries

Through your role as a mentor you are likely to get opportunities to develop better emotional intelligence abilities, but you should also bear in mind that you are not required to solve all of your mentees' problems and if you feel that the issues they are facing are too much for you to be able to help them with you should signpost them to the university counselling service, medical centre or other professional service for specialist advice. Although this may not feel very satisfactory because you may perceive that you are simply passing on a problem, it is better to signpost your mentees to professional support and to keep yourself safe rather than trying to help but realising that you are ill-equipped to deal with their issues. The following points are tips to help you set and maintain boundaries in your mentoring relationship:

- **Know your limits:** In order to understand your boundaries as a mentor it is crucial to have a clear understanding of your role. This should be outlined to you either when you are recruited as a mentor or in pre-mentoring training. It is important that you convey this information to your mentees. In fact, reaching a mutual understanding of the mentoring role and its limits may be one of the first things that you do together (see the mentoring contract below).
- **Tune in to your feelings:** Try to be aware of when you are uncomfortable with a conversation. Perhaps try to rate the conversation from 1 to 5, with 1 being easy and relaxed conversation and 5 being conversation which feels very uncomfortable or difficult. Any conversations rated 3 or above may be ones that you need to reflect on and think about whether you need to signpost your mentees elsewhere (see the reflective journal entry).
- **Be direct:** It can be difficult to do this, but with practice it is easier to be direct with your mentees if you feel that they have crossed a boundary. Phrases such as 'I don't think this is an area which I can advise you on' or 'This isn't really within the remit of our relationship' can be helpful in making a boundary clear.
- **Give yourself permission:** Often we can feel pressure to stretch our boundaries in order to reach out and help someone else, but this is not a healthy approach, so try to give yourself permission to set clear boundaries and reinforce them when you feel they are being stretched (look back at the boundary circle in Chapter 2).
- **Practise self-awareness:** Often when we are busy we can lose touch with ourselves. As a mentor it is useful to take time out regularly to reflect on yourself and check whether the mentoring relationship has changed and whether your boundaries are still intact. This may be something you can do in a feedback session with a mentor co-ordinator.
- **Consider your past and your present:** Review your past study and support experiences and then think about the situation you are in now. Make sure that you are giving enough time to your own study as well as time to your mentees.
- **Make self-care a priority:** Remind yourself of your own goals in relation to your study so that you don't lose sight of this by helping others too much. Remember that an important aspect of being a mentor is modelling good study behaviours.
- **Seek support:** If you find that your boundaries are slipping, seek support from a more experienced mentor or mentor co-ordinator at the university.

Mentoring contract

The points above give you guidance to help you maintain your boundaries within a mentoring relationship. You may also find it helpful to develop with your mentees a mentoring agreement which sets out what they can expect and what goes beyond the remit of the mentoring relationship.

Mentoring agreement

We will meet ... a week for ... minutes throughout terms one and two of this academic year. We will meet in a mutually agreed public space on the campus.

I (mentee's name)_____ agree to:

be on time and prepared for each mentoring session

email 24 hours in advance if I cannot make a mentoring session

accept that I am responsible for my own learning and results

keep all discussions from within the mentoring relationship confidential.

Signed_____

Date_____

I (mentor's name)_____ agree to:

be on time and prepared for each mentoring session

email 24 hours in advance if I cannot make a mentoring session

support you with your studies and life at university

keep all discussions from within the mentoring relationship confidential.

Signed_____

Date_____

Listen actively

Active listening encourages you to focus on what your mentees are saying and avoid directing them into a particular course of action, but allow them time to work out what is right for them. This can sometimes be a very difficult thing to do, especially if you feel that you know what the best course of action would be. However, as individuals we all need to come to our own decisions, even if they turn out to be wrong. Therefore a key aspect of mentor training is helping you to recognise the nature of your relationship with your mentees, which is usually described as friendly and helpful, but with awareness of your limitations and a responsibility to signpost mentees to professional support rather than trying to take on complex issues single-handedly.

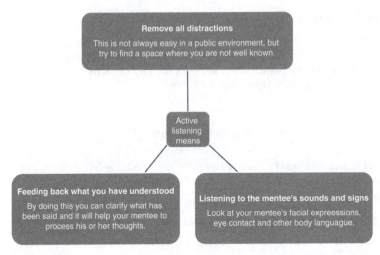

Remove all distractions
This is not always easy in a public environment, but try to find a space where you are not well known.

Active listening means

Feeding back what you have understood
By doing this you can clarify what has been said and it will help your mentee to process his or her thoughts.

Listening to the mentee's sounds and signs
Look at your mentee's facial expreessions, eye contact and other body languague.

Active listening

Authenticity

One of the key advantages which peer mentors have over other people with supportive roles within the university is that there is a greater sense of proximity and authenticity from a peer mentor. As a student you have recently experienced similar things to your mentees so you are in a really good position to help and support. One thing to be careful of, though, is the tendency to compare yourself to your mentees. Although you may have had similar experiences recently, we all react differently, so it may be useful to share some of your experiences, but do not expect that your mentees will react the same as you.

Support and supervision

In any helping relationship which has an emphasis on interpersonal relationships, there may be a need for support and supervision from time to time. There may be things that come up within a mentoring relationship which trouble you and which you may want support with. The support and supervision which mentors receive vary significantly from scheme to scheme, but it is important that you know there are people to turn to if you feel that you need support. Information about this should be part of your training and should also be available in literature and web information at your university.

Recognising mental health issues

Awareness of mental health conditions has improved significantly in recent years. It is now widely known that one in four of us will at some point in our lives experience some form of mental health disorder. We also know that mental health conditions most commonly surface when a person is aged between 18 and 25, so students are a particularly vulnerable group. This is often exacerbated by the fact that university life can be complex and stressful, with the added pressure of financial hardship for many students. This will mean that there are likely to be some mentees who have mental health issues. However, they may not have been formally diagnosed, either because the condition has developed recently or because they may be reluctant to get a diagnosis due to the persistent stigma which surrounds mental illness.

There are certain things which indicate mental health issues (adapted from the MIND website):

- poor physical health
- poor hygiene
- tiredness
- absence or lateness
- poor concentration
- anxiety
- withdrawal
- attention-seeking behaviour.

If your mentee shows any of these signs it may or may not indicate mental ill-health. Do not jump to premature conclusions, but make sure your mentee knows where to go for professional support should they need it. It is also useful to bear in mind the five steps to wellbeing which the NHS recommends for all of us. You can use these to give practical suggestions to your mentee of ways they can make positive changes in their life.

Five ways	What students can do
Connect	Try to join a group or a club so that you have a feeling of belonging. The students' union will have a list of all the clubs and societies at your university.
Take notice	Be mindful when you are in action such as cooking or eating. Focus on what you are doing and try to keep other thoughts at bay.
Keep learning	As a student you are already in a learning environment, but you may want to learn something non-assessed, such as dance, music or a language.
Give	Give your time to others in any way that you can. At university there are always lots of volunteering opportunities which students can get involved in.
Be active	Get out and do exercise. It doesn't have to be formal or organised, but it is good for your mind to do physical activity.

Building your own resilience

Mentors can play a vital role in supporting their mentees in stressful times, but it is important to look after yourself and check that you are not taking on too much of someone else's stress. If you start to feel stressed, try to take a step back and look after your own wellbeing. There are all sorts of ways of doing this, including taking exercise, listening to or playing music, dancing, cooking or meditating. Essentially, it is important to make time for yourself. This will enable you to be calm and relaxed and therefore able to offer more support to your mentees. Regarding mental health and supporting others with mental health issues, there is lots of useful information on the NHS and MIND websites.

Conclusion

This chapter has looked in detail at the interpersonal mature of mentoring and the challenges that this presents. It has given you some practical strategies for working closely with others at an emotional level. It has also shown you that by doing this work you will be building up the highly valued skill of emotional intelligence. The chapter has given you a range of practical tools with which to work with your mentees to support them through the usual ups and downs of student life. It has also shown you how to set and maintain boundaries if you feel that your mentees need more professional support.

Key points from the chapter

- It is important to set and maintain clear boundaries.
- Listen actively to your mentees.
- Do not try to solve mentees' issues which are beyond your expertise.
- Mentoring will develop your emotional intelligence.

Troubleshooting

By the end of this chapter you will:

- be aware of the problems that might arise when acting as a mentor
- be able to apply strategies to deal with difficult or challenging situations
- be aware of the boundaries of the mentoring role and when to refer your mentee for further help and guidance.

Being a mentor is usually a very rewarding experience, with the mentor feeling good not only about the help that they are able to offer others but also about the additional skills that they themselves gain. The relationship between mentors and mentees is unique in that the mentor will have invested time and energy in the scheme with the expectation that mentees will be equally committed. While in the majority of cases things run smoothly and both parties are happy with the way things go, unfortunately this is not always the case. Mentors can become frustrated or disappointed by the failure of mentees to engage with them, or by the way in which they behave when they do. But, as with any relationship, things will not always run smoothly and the reasons for this will not always be clear-cut or easy to resolve. This chapter provides a series of difficult scenarios which mentors may face within their role. It enables you to think about how you might respond and makes suggestions about how a mentor can deal with these types of situation and where to seek further sources of support.

Lack of engagement

One of the most frustrating things for a mentor is the failure of their mentees to engage with the programme. You may find that your school has an opt-in policy where first-year students are given information about the mentoring scheme and have to make a conscious decision to join it. Other schools will have an opt-out system where all first-year students are automatically enrolled in the scheme and allocated a mentor on arrival. In both cases, timing is a major factor as, at the beginning of the academic year, freshers are bombarded with information both by email and on paper. This 'information overload' at such a stressful time can be overwhelming and it is only natural that they will focus on the most important things first, such as accommodation, finances, timetabling, settling in and making new friends. In the first few weeks, that first essay deadline seems a long way off and students will not yet know what difficulties they might face in the weeks ahead. Because of this, making contact with their mentor may be the last thing on their mind.

Do not be surprised, therefore, if students do not rush to join up, or, if they are automatically enrolled, they do not respond to your attempts to contact them. Try to remember how it felt when you first arrived, with so many practical things you had to deal with, as well as issues concerned with living away from home, possibly for the first time.

Contact

You will probably have received your mentor training before the start of the academic year so you will have met your fellow mentors. It is a good idea to create a social media presence for the group so that mentors can communicate between themselves initially, and then with mentees once they arrive on campus, or, even better, before they arrive. Mentees report that they tend not to respond to random emails from people they do not know and are far more likely to engage via social media. A visible presence during Freshers' Week and at school induction events is another good way of promoting the scheme and making contact with mentees.

As well as informal events, it is a good idea to make arrangements with module convenors to go into key lectures at the beginning of term and speak about the scheme for a few minutes. You could also prepare a slide in PowerPoint (see below), giving all the basic information about mentoring which lecturers could show at the beginning or end of their lectures and which could be posted on to their module virtual learning environment (VLE). In this way, students will have settled not only into university but also into the subject and will be beginning to think about their first assignments.

Peer mentors are available to help students enrolled on this module with:

- sharing notes from lectures
- preparing for seminars
- discussing course content
- following up on seminar discussions
- explaining assignment briefs.

For Further information

Email peermentoring@anyuni.ac.uk
Look up the webpage at www.anyunipeermentoring.ac.uk
Check out our Facebook page at anyunipeermentoring

The way in which the peer mentoring scheme is presented is also of vital importance. No one wants to admit that they are struggling, so if mentees feel that having a mentor is remedial they may be reluctant to engage with their mentor. However, if having a mentor is seen as the norm, and part of a 'success strategy', mentees are far more likely to want to get involved and find ways of making sure that they do as well as they possibly can.

Attendance and responsibility

There is a natural tendency for students to want to be 'friends' with fellow students, but the relationship between mentor and mentee is unique in that there is an inherent distance between them. This is because, although both you and your mentee are students enrolled on the same programme, you will be at a more advanced stage of the process and therefore more knowledgeable both in terms of the subject matter and the discipline as a whole. In addition, because you have been recruited and trained to carry out a specific role, you become part of the establishment with responsibilities towards your department and the university. With this unique change in status come additional responsibilities, and mentors report that they often feel personally responsible for the initial and ongoing engagement and academic progression of their mentees.

However, the progression of your mentees is *not* your responsibility. Your role is to enable them as far as you can, but, ultimately, the decision to engage with you and your advice must be theirs. If your mentees fail to respond when you contact them, or do not turn up to prearranged mentoring sessions, this could be for any number of reasons, such as illness or work commitments, or just forgetting about the appointment. On the other hand, it might just be that they decided not to attend and did not bother to let you know. Mentees who do not notify mentors in advance of group sessions report that they were not concerned as they assumed that others would be there and so they would not be missed. This is obviously frustrating as you will have planned for the number of mentees that you were expecting and may have to adapt your plans on the spot to make the session work. You need to always have a plan B ready just in case you end up with only one or two students instead of the larger number you were hoping for.

For one-to-one mentoring sessions the situation is different, and mentees who cannot attend should feel that they are under more of an obligation to let you know if they are unable to make it, unless perhaps there has been a last-minute emergency. In this case, they should make every effort to contact you as soon as possible after the event to explain their absence.

Another, more positive reason for mentees not attending mentoring sessions is that they do not need any help. Mentors report that some mentees attend for the first few weeks only and then do not contact their mentors again. Mentees often report that the initial sessions were very useful and that they did not feel the need for further advice or support. In cases like this the mentoring relationship is considered a success in that the role of the mentor is to enable the mentee, rather than to make them become dependent.

In order to avoid misunderstandings and the possibility of the mentoring relationship breaking down, it is important to lay out some ground rules at the beginning which include the issues of time keeping and communication. As stated above, as a fellow student, you would assume that your mentees would view and treat you as such. But, as a mentor, you become part of the establishment and therefore mentees may not feel that they need to let you know they are not going to attend, in the same way that students sometimes fail to attend lectures and seminars and do not let the lecturer know in advance and yet later approach them for information or notes about what was covered in the session.

In order to avoid this happening, it is a good idea to send your mentees a reminder message via email, text or social media before the meeting, asking them to confirm that they can make it. Ground rules around making and breaking appointments should also be discussed with your mentees at the initial meeting.

Example

Ground rules:

- Mentors will arrange meetings once a week at a regular time and place.
- Mentees will try to attend all arranged meetings.
- Mentors and mentees will notify each other via email of changes in meeting arrangements at least one day in advance of the meeting wherever possible.
- Mentees will notify their mentor via email if they no longer require mentoring.

If you have arranged a group mentoring session or a one-to-one meeting and the mentee(s) do not turn up, you should make contact with them as soon as possible after the event. This is not only so that the meeting can be rearranged but also to prevent the relationship from breaking down. Mentees report that they sometimes feel unable to return to the group, or contact their mentor, because they feel awkward or embarrassed because they did not let them know they could not attend the original session. If you can keep the lines of communication open, it is more likely that they will stay with the scheme and continue to benefit from it.

Activity 7.1

- You have a meeting arranged with a mentee or a group of mentees to go over a specific issue, but either only a few or no one turns up. You feel rather annoyed because you have spent quite a lot of time preparing for the session. How would you react to this and what would you write in your message to those who were due to attend?

- Tom came to the very first session and has not appeared since. You are concerned about his attitude and feel that he should attend because he seems to be in great need of help and support. Do you have the attitude of 'live and let live' or would you feel that you need to do more?

Boundaries of role

As an academic peer mentor you will deal primarily with issues surrounding your mentees' academic progression. However, it is inevitable that there will be times when personal issues impact on a mentee's work. You are not expected to act as a counsellor or confidante, but there will be times when the discussions cross over into personal concerns. These could be anything from a lack of confidence, a noisy flatmate making it difficult for your mentee to study, illness or disability which means that additional time is needed to complete assignments, housing or financial problems, or more complex relationship or mental health issues. In some cases you may be able to give advice, such as to suggest working in the library rather than at home, or pointing them towards a particular piece of software that makes referencing quicker. Mentees may suffer from anxiety when assignments are due or when exams are looming. In cases like this, you can empathise and suggest coping strategies, as well as practical help in terms of revision planning and time management.

However, there may be times when you have more serious concerns about your mentee's mental health. Although you will have been trained to recognise the signs as a mentor, you are not expected to deal with this yourself and under no circumstances should you attempt to do so. It is possible that there are underlying factors that you are not aware of and no matter how well meaning you may be, your actions could cause more harm than good. If your mentee raises the subject themselves, you could suggest that they contact their GP or relevant support teams within the university. Of course, in order to be able to do this, you will need to make sure that you are familiar with all that your university has to offer in terms of support and be able to provide your mentee with the contact details as appropriate. In all cases, if you have concerns about the wellbeing of a mentee, you should approach the mentoring coordinator in your school for advice. In an emergency situation where you believe that the mentee is a danger to themselves or others, you are under an obligation to immediately speak to a member of staff and report the situation. Where possible you should seek the permission of your mentee to break confidence. If it is out of hours, you should contact your university's campus security or, if that fails, the emergency services.

Activity 7.2

- You are mentoring a girl who is unhealthily slim, and you have noticed that since Christmas she has become even skinnier. She wears baggy clothes to hide this but it is obvious to you that there is a problem. You are worried that she may end up doing serious damage to her body. What should you do?

- You are mentoring a boy whose father passed away at the beginning of the year. Since then he has become increasingly dependent on drugs and alcohol, which he used to enjoy recreationally. Now he needs to smoke drugs or drink alcohol in the morning. He has begun to appear dishevelled and to neglect his personal hygiene. What should you do?

Helping those who help themselves

There may be times when you are working with a mentee and you feel that they are not taking their studies seriously, instead expecting you to show them an easy, quick route to success. With others, it may seem that although you are asked for, and give, advice, your suggestions are ignored so the mentees' problems continue. This can be very challenging and you may end up feeling that you are wasting your time trying to help someone who is not willing to help themselves.

It is only natural that your willingness to help will have its limits, because people are less likely to want to help those whose own behaviour caused the problem (Frey and Gaertner, 1986). It is easy to feel good about helping someone who is not at fault, but what happens when you feel that your mentee is entirely to blame for their poor marks or their failure to engage with particular aspects of their course? In situations like this you will probably experience negative feelings when your mentee asks for help and expects you to help them solve the problems that have occurred because of things they themselves have or have not done.

However, things might not always be as clear-cut as they first seem. Take, for instance, the case of a mentor whose mentee insisted on an urgent appointment because they needed help with referencing and were in a rush to get a train home that same day. The mentor agreed but was rather annoyed because they themselves were particularly busy, and felt that the mentee should have planned their time better and prioritised their studies over taking time out. At the meeting it turned out that the mentee was having to rush home for a family emergency and needed to submit quickly as they would be unable to do so from home. This example highlights the need for good communication.

In other situations, too, things may not be simple, and what may appear to be a failure to engage, or take advice, may in fact be due to other pressures or commitments. This can be very challenging for mentors, because you will need to put aside your feelings of frustration or possibly resentment and try to read between the lines to see what is really going on. It is possible, of course, that your mentee just does not want to engage with the scheme and is happy working alone. If this were the case they would probably not be attending the sessions or communicating with you at all. The fact that they are means that they have acknowledged that they need help. Because of this, it is worth persevering to get to the bottom of whatever the problem might be and then trying to find a strategy to deal with it. This might include making suggestions about engaging with other services within the university as appropriate, such as academic skills support or counselling.

Activity 7.3

- David came to you with feedback from his assignment which said that his referencing style was incorrect. You went through a few examples with him, booked him into a referencing workshop and said that if he redid the references and bibliography you would be happy to go through them with him to make sure he understood what to do next time. You did not hear from David again until the day before his next essay was due, when he asked you to check his referencing for him, saying that he had not had time to do as you suggested; nor had he attended the workshop. How would you handle this situation?

- Carl seems to be quite moody and uncooperative. Although he attends most of the group mentoring sessions, he sits on his own and does not join in any discussions or take part in any group activity. You have heard from others that he spends most of his time in his room playing computer games and often misses lectures and seminars. You are concerned by Carl's attitude and lack of commitment. Should you intervene? If so, how?

Miscommunication

Mentoring does not always have to take place face to face. Any communication between you and your mentees, such as an email, text or social media message, counts. This form of mentoring is particularly useful if your mentees are off campus, have a quick question or want to clarify something fairly straightforward. In fact, having a Facebook group for you and your fellow mentors to communicate with the mentees in your school is a really useful way of keeping in touch and sharing information. Posting details about particular topics which relate to core modules along with frequently asked questions also allows mentees who do not otherwise engage to benefit from your advice.

However, communicating in writing as opposed to face to face can be problematic because, without the tone of voice or body language, words can easily be misinterpreted. Imagine, for instance, that you were face to face with somebody and asked a question. If they answered simply 'yes' but nodded and smiled at the same time, that would be fine. But if you sent an email asking the same question and the reply that came back was simply 'yes', you would have no way of knowing if the person was being pleasant, curt or dismissive.

Therefore it is really important to think about how your written words will be received. It is always worth taking the time to start with a salutation of some kind, even if it is just something very simple and informal like 'Hi', and to end the message with a closing phrase, such as 'Best wishes' or 'See you soon'. Equally, when you read messages from mentees, it might be that they seem curt, even rude, but this is not necessarily the case. It is always worth trying to imagine how the same thing might sound if you were hearing instead of reading it. Things to consider are the level of formality which you wish to convey to your mentees and possibly the cultural dynamic between you and your mentees, which could lead to confusion.

As discussed above, there may be times when mentees are not engaging with you, or they do not attend sessions that you have arranged, or indeed that they have requested, without letting you know in advance. In cases like this you will need to contact them and make the point that it is not acceptable to waste your time, but it is important to do so in a way that does not discourage them from contacting you again. Finding the right words to convey that, first, they should have contacted you because your time has been wasted, and, second, that it is okay and you are happy to rearrange is not easy. Keeping the message in draft form for a while and then coming back to it is a useful way of checking how it might be read when it is received.

Activity 7.4

- You and your fellow mentors arranged a session for your mentees and only three out of ten attended. Draft a message to those who did not attend that makes the point that you would like them to let you know if they cannot make it in future and encourages them to attend next week.

- You had arranged to meet a mentee for a one-to-one discussion but they did not turn up. Later that day you received an email that said 'Soz, up late. Tomorrow, same time?' What would you say in reply?

Conclusion

This chapter has considered some of the problems that you might face within the mentoring relationship. These range from the failure of mentees to fully engage with you and the mentoring scheme, issues of communication and being able to recognise mental health issues. Not all mentees will fully engage with the scheme, but this does not mean that you have failed as a mentor. Mentees who only come to see you intermittently, or in the first few weeks of each term, are probably coping well, which means that you have enabled them to be independent. Others may regularly attend mentoring sessions, or contact you online throughout their first year as different challenges arise.

It is therefore important to build your own resilience as a mentor so that you can withstand some of the common difficulties which can arise. Various resilience scales have been developed which can be used as a measure of a person's 'bounce-back' and adaptability. You might find it interesting to review your own resilience by using the scale below, which is based on Connor and Davidson's (2003) work. On this scale, 0 indicates no resilience at all and 4 indicates a very high level of resilience.

Resilience indicators	0	1	2	3	4
I am able to adapt to change					
I can deal with whatever comes up					
Past success gives me confidence for new challenges					
I see the humorous side of things					
I tend to bounce back after difficult times or illness					
I think things happen for a reason					
I know where to turn for help					
I like challenges					
I work to achieve my goals					
I take pride in my achievements					
I have a strong sense of purpose					
I take a lead in problem solving					

Some of the challenges that may be faced have been discussed in this chapter, but remember that you do not have to deal with these, or any other issues that might come up, alone. You will have the support and guidance of your mentoring co-ordinator, who will either provide training and resources to help you or take ownership of the problem themselves.

Key points from this chapter

- Not all mentees will engage with you, but this does not mean that you have failed as a mentor.
- Online communication needs to be carefully managed to avoid misunderstandings.
- You are not required to deal with every problem that arises, and you should take advice if you have any concerns.

What Skills Do Mentors Gain?

By the end of this chapter you will:

- be aware of the employability skills associated with being a mentor
- be aware of the impact of mentoring on your own learning
- be able to effectively communicate the skills developed through mentoring to prospective employers.

This chapter will concentrate on the way in which the transferable skills gained and enhanced through acting as a mentor relate to your personal and professional development. Employability skills are now accepted as an important part of a degree programme, and being a mentor is one of the ways in which you can gain, enhance and demonstrate the additional skills that employers are looking for. In order to highlight the variety and range of transferable skills that are involved in being a mentor, this chapter will take an in-depth look at what mentors do in practical terms and map it against specific employability descriptors. As we know, mentoring is a reciprocal relationship in which mentors can gain as much from the experience of mentoring as mentees do from being mentored. In fact, Donelan (1999) asserts that mentors are the 'real winners' in the mentor–mentee relationship and that they gain far more from the relationship than the mentees. This is because being a mentor requires you to call upon a wide range of academic, professional and personal skills, most of which you will already be using in other areas of your life without realising their importance or transferability. As you will see in Chapter 9, reflection enables you to recognise what these skills are and how they relate to the world of employment. In this chapter you will be encouraged to think about the skills that you already have and how they can be applied in both mentoring and employment situations. You will also think about the additional skills that you will acquire through your training and practice as a mentor.

The second part of the chapter will consider the way in which the application of these skills also relates to your own academic progression and can be used to enhance and promote your own learning through the processes of revision, explanation and collaborative learning.

Mentoring and employability

Mentoring is an excellent way of developing your employability skills. However, it is important to recognise what these skills are so that you can demonstrate them to prospective employers when making applications and at interview.

A recent survey of Kent graduates showed that 91% of mentors achieve graduate level jobs as opposed to 82% of students generally (University of Kent, 2016). This is a clear indication that employers recognise and value the skills learned through mentoring. It also demonstrates how important it is that mentors themselves recognise those skills and include them on CVs and job applications.

In fact, many universities ask mentors to apply to be a mentor in the same way as they would apply for other employment, and they provide a person specification and job description.

On a practical level, you will find that being a mentor gives you the opportunity to develop a range of graduate employability skills and provides you with concrete examples that can be included in job applications or discussed at interview.

Graduate employability skills

Based on a number of surveys on the skills required by graduates undertaken by Microsoft, Target Jobs, the BBC, Prospects and other organisations, the skills which were deemed most important are:

Oral communication: expressing ideas clearly and confidently in speech

Teamwork: working confidently within a group

Commercial awareness: seeing the 'bigger picture', the realities affecting the organisation

Analysing and investigating: gathering information to establish facts and principles, problem solving

Initiative/self-motivation: acting on initiative, identifying opportunities and being proactive in putting forward ideas and solutions

Drive: being determined to get things done, making things happen and constantly looking for better ways of doing things

Written communication: expressing yourself clearly in writing

Planning and organisation: planning activities and carrying them through effectively

Flexibility: adapting to changing situations and environments

Time management: managing time effectively, prioritising tasks and working to deadlines.

Employability skills gained through mentoring

As a mentor you will be able to develop and enhance your employability skills, but it is vital that you are aware of this process. To help you see your skills as they develop, the table below gives examples of how mentoring develops key employability skills. There is space beside to allow you to think about specific examples you have gained through mentoring which have improved your skills in these areas.

Skills	How mentoring develops these skills
Communication: Involves listening, understanding and speaking clearly; effective persuasion and negotiation skills; and being able to demonstrate empathy, assertiveness and tact in order to establish and use networks and share information and ideas. Listening to and understanding what is both said and unsaid is a key part of working with mentees as there may be times when they are unable to articulate what the problem is, or know what it is that they need to ask.	Mentors can use their own experience in these situations, having been in the same position themselves. Mentors will also recognise that new students may not have the technical vocabulary required by the discipline and will therefore need to communicate ideas in clearer language.
Planning: Managing time and priorities; being resourceful, taking the initiative and making decisions; delivering training, motivating others and giving feedback; reporting on progress and outcomes, and demonstrating resilience in order to establish clear and attainable project goals and deliverables.	One of the key roles of a mentor is to motivate and inspire others through example and to be able to communicate that experience through both pre-planned structured sessions and ad hoc interactions. Being able to plan ahead is essential as a mentor. As a student and a mentor, your first priority must be your own studies and you may also have other commitments, such as employment, family or caring responsibilities. It is therefore important to manage your time effectively and plan ahead, being aware of key times when you will be under pressure so that you can work around these.
Organisation: Closely related to planning, these skills involve thinking scenarios through before they happen and putting things in place so that work runs smoothly.	As well as the regular sessions that you will have as agreed with your mentees, you will need to communicate with them to arrange times and venues, discuss the content of sessions and prepare appropriate material. This may involve liaising with your fellow mentees or members of the academic team to find out what has been covered that week, booking a room, gathering resources and preparing. Whether you are meeting groups of mentees or talking one to one with a mentee, you will probably also need to go back over your own module notes to consolidate your understanding of the topic so that you are in a position to explain it clearly to your mentees.

Skills	How mentoring develops these skills
Training and development: In the modern work environment, continuous professional development is expected from employees because it is seen as an essential way for workers and organisations to maintain their relevance and respond to a changing world.	As well as your initial training sessions, you may be offered the opportunity of further development to enhance your skills. You may feel that you are well equipped to start being a mentor after attending the initial compulsory training, but making time to attend additional sessions, if they are offered, will allow you to develop your skills still further and put them into context. In this way you can consolidate what you have learned and recognise how to apply it to other situations.
Reflection: This means the ability to stand back from a situation and review what went well and what needs to be improved. Reflection enables learning based on experience to take place. This is either done formally in professions such as teaching, nursing and social work or informally in other professions, but the ability to reflect is highly valued in the workplace.	At the end of a mentoring session it is useful to spend a little time reviewing how it went; making notes on how many mentees attended; the main issue(s) discussed; how the group functioned or, if a one-to-one session, how the dynamic worked between you and your mentee; any areas that you need to prepare or develop for the next session; and notes so that you can provide feedback if required to do so by your department.
Problem solving: This includes the ability to define the problem and its contributing factors; make realistic decisions and action plans; develop creative, innovative and/or practical solutions; implement and monitor solutions; and evaluate processes and outcomes in order to apply a range of strategies to problem solving and personal understanding. Advising on pastoral issues requires an in-depth knowledge of the institution and its practices as well as the skill of recognising personal limitations. There is further discussion on the types of problem you might face as a mentor, and how to deal with them in Chapter 7.	As a mentor, you will find yourself dealing with a range of issues, some of which may be unfamiliar to you. While the primary focus will be on academic issues, you may also need to address the pastoral issues that impact on your mentees' academic progression. The act of delivering guidance on course-specific and academic skills issues means that mentors' own learning and expertise are consolidated as the act of explaining requires enhanced knowledge of the subject.
Team working: This includes the ability to work effectively with different ages, genders, races and religions; to clarify and establish team roles to perform agreed tasks; to give and receive effective feedback; and to deal with conflict or misunderstandings within a team	The ability to establish team roles to perform agreed tasks is a key part of the mentor–mentee relationship. The mentor initially takes the lead role but seeks to encourage the mentee to become part of the team, the learning community and the discipline as a whole as the relationship progresses. Mentors also work with a team of fellow mentors, who are themselves part

Skills	How mentoring develops these skills
and recognise personal strengths and weaknesses in order to be able to work effectively with others to complete tasks and achieve results.	of a larger team offering various forms of support within the university as a whole. As well as working with fellow mentors you will inevitably interact with mentees from a range of backgrounds and learning capabilities. The ability to recognise, work with and resolve these differences while at the same time respecting them are crucial aspects of team working.
Leadership: This is more than just being in charge of a team. Being a good leader involves having a solid vision and understanding of the end goal and the ability to bring together the skills needed to achieve it. This means being able to motivate, guide, inspire, listen to and persuade those around you as well as demonstrate resilience when things go wrong. In the workplace the application of these skills is a key part of any successful team, whether as part of the management structure or as a team member.	In a mentoring relationship you will act as the 'leader' and your mentee will be guided by you, not just in terms of academic instruction but also by the example of your attitude and behaviour. It is possible that at times you will be faced with a lack of enthusiasm from your mentees. It is important to recognise that this is not a personal affront but instead perhaps indicates a reluctance to acknowledge or accept that the help being offered is relevant. The attitude of the mentor is crucial in the development of team-spirit and to facilitate students working together collaboratively in a mutually advantageous relationship. This will enable you to achieve the end goal of academic success which you both share.

Activity 8.1

Look at the following case studies, based on real experiences which mentors have encountered. Think about how the experiences that they describe could be rewritten to display specific employability skills. The first one is done as an example for you. Try to do the other two yourself.

Case study 1

A mentor reported a situation where she felt that her mentee was under a lot of stress. It was manifesting itself in mood swings and arguments with other students. The mentor felt that she wanted to help her mentee through this difficult situation but she was unsure of how to do this so she attended an extra session put on by her university entitled 'Recognising and supporting wellbeing', which gave her some practical strategies and reminded her of her boundaries. After this she was able to support the mentee so that he accessed counselling support, and she reflected on her own strategies for dealing with stress.

Rewrite:

I have a commitment to my own professional development; for example, as a mentor at university I was required to support another student who was having a difficult time. Although at first I felt under-equipped to help, I applied for extra training, which taught me some useful strategies, and I was able to put them into practice.

Case study 2

A mentor was approached by a mentee who was looking for guidance on a specific aspect of their course. Although the mentor didn't feel able to answer that question herself, she was aware that the university offered workshops on specific aspects of learning. After making some enquiries she was able to advise her mentee how to sign up for the workshop.

Rewrite:

Case study 3

A team of mentors from the same school found that many of their mentees were experiencing problems with referencing, so they worked together to create a workshop. Within the workshop, mentees broke into small groups to work on activities which used course-specific material. Afterwards the mentors collated the worksheets and uploaded them to the virtual learning environment (VLE) so that other mentees could refer to these examples.

Rewrite:

Mentoring: a two-way process

As you have seen above, there are benefits for mentors on a personal and vocational level. The range of benefits includes:

- increased self-esteem, motivation and confidence
- increased sense of direction and purpose
- acquisition and development of study skills
- improved academic achievement
- a higher level of commitment and application to their studies
- help in combating underachievement
- the opportunity to work with a positive role model
- increased awareness of the opportunities available to them
- increased employability skills.

Activity 8.2

Locate an advertisement for a job which relates to your chosen career path and make a list of the attributes and skills listed in the job description and person specification.

Compare your list to the employability skills gained through mentoring, and consider the ways in which being a mentor might assist you in both making an application for the post and fulfilling the role in the workplace.

From your point of view as a mentor, the role also provides new challenges and the opportunity to develop new skills. You should benefit in particular in terms of:

- having an opportunity to participate in training and development opportunities
- increasing your personal effectiveness as a result of your experiences as a mentor
- experiencing the satisfaction of helping others to develop and achieve their goals
- being able to use the experiences on your CV to enhance your career prospects
- consolidating your own learning as a result of revisiting and explaining key concepts of your modules.

Personal skills audit

The skills discussed above are all relevant to your academic development. As you work through the personal skills audit below, rate your skills from 1 to 5 with 1 as the lowest and 5 as the highest. As you go through the questions, think about how the items listed relate both to the workplace and to your academic progression, and note down examples for each. For instance, when you think about communicating, you might find examples where you have to listen and/or speak in lectures or seminars with a diverse group of people; team working might involve working on a group project or presentation; problem solving could be understanding and planning an essay or working on a practical project or report; and planning and organisation relates to planning and organising your time. Revisit this chart from time to time to check your progress.

Personal skills audit					
1. Communicating					
	1	2	3	4	5
Listening, understanding and speaking clearly					
Persuading and negotiating effectively					
Demonstrating empathy, assertiveness and tact					

Understanding the needs of others					
Establishing relationships and using networks					
Sharing information and proposing ideas					
2. Team working					
	1	2	3	4	5
Working effectively with different ages, genders, races and religions					
Working effectively with others to complete tasks and achieve results					
Clarifying team roles and performing agreed tasks					
Giving and receiving constructive feedback					
Dealing with conflict or misunderstandings within a team					
Recognising own strengths and limitations					
3. Problem solving					
	1	2	3	4	5
Defining the problem and contributing factors					
Developing creative, innovative and/or practical solutions					
Making realistic decisions and action plans					
Applying a range of strategies to problem solving					
Implementing and monitoring solutions					
Evaluating processes and outcomes					
4. Planning and organising					
	1	2	3	4	5
Establishing clear and attainable project goals and deliverables					
Managing time and priorities – setting goals					
Being resourceful, taking initiative and making decisions					
Training, developing, motivating and giving feedback					
Reporting on progress and outcomes					
Demonstrating resilience					

Enhancing your own learning

As well as transferable and employability skills, being a mentor will help you consolidate your own learning because, in order to explain key concepts to your mentees, you have to go back over potentially challenging parts of the topic and mentally organise them. Through doing this you are engaging with the material at a deeper level than you perhaps did originally and this solidifies your own understanding of it (Micari et al., 2005). It also creates a mutually beneficial relationship which helps both mentors and mentees to become more thoughtful and engaged learners, as well as underpinning the idea that obtaining knowledge is, in itself, a communal activity within most disciplines (Kelly, 2002).

As we explained in Chapter 5, although there will be times when you are asked to repeat or clarify module material, your role is different from the lecturer or seminar leader in that you are not *teaching* these concepts. Instead, it is likely that you will already have been taught and examined on the material, so in effect both you and your mentees are *re*-learning it. You will thus engage in what Johnston and Johnston (1991) term 'collaborative learning', where both you and your mentees are 'learners', albeit at different stages and levels of understanding. This is different from 'instructional learning', which is when the learner (in this case the mentee) is a passive recipient of the information (Brown et al., 2014). The collaborative learning process goes beyond the academic issues and becomes a way of developing interpersonal and employability skills, such as team working and communication.

Mentors from across all disciplines report that they have benefited from being part of the mentoring programme. Comments include:

> When I was helping my mentees to plan their essays, it made me really think about the way that I wrote myself. It was really helpful because I actually changed the way I do things because I had to think about it more so I could explain it. (Phillip, psychology mentor)

> I had to revise the material from last year before I went to meet my mentees. I had forgotten a lot of it so it was really good that I was forced to go back over it! (Lenny, biosciences mentor)

> I used to be really nervous about giving presentations, but I gave quite a few to my mentees and that helped me feel a lot more confident when it came to doing them in my own seminars. (Joshua, classics mentor)

> I used to be really disorganised but, as a mentor, my mentees were relying on me and I wanted to set a good example. It forced me to sort out my time better and this has made things much easier for my own work too. I actually wrote a revision timetable this year which has really helped me to fit it all in. (Megan, social sciences mentor)

> Being a mentor made me mix with lots of different people. Sometimes it was challenging, but the training showed me how not to be judgemental and, actually, I learned a lot about myself as well as about them. (Emily, engineering mentor)

As you can see, as well as enhancing your own academic abilities through the revision of discipline-specific module content, mentoring offers you the opportunity to develop and enhance your own study strategies and time management. Because of the need to prepare and then present material in mentoring sessions, you will also practise your writing and presentation skills, which will increase your confidence and have a positive impact on your own assessed work.

Conclusion

This chapter has demonstrated the ways in which being a mentor is useful from an employability point of view, and considered how the skills and attributes required to fulfil the role are similar to those that are most sought after by graduate employers. The aim of the chapter was to demonstrate the ways in which you can draw upon your experiences as a mentor when completing job applications and in interview situations by offering concrete examples of where and how you gained specific skills.

As well as highlighting the employability skills associated with mentoring, this chapter has considered the way in which being a mentor can be used to consolidate your own learning in terms of academic content and study skills.

Key points

- Being a mentor offers the opportunity to learn and enhance the skills required by graduate employers.
- Recognising where and when you use and develop these attributes gives you concrete examples to include in application letters and interview discussions.
- Reflection is a key part of mentoring.

Reflecting on the Experience of Being a Mentor

9

By the end of this chapter you will:

- have an understanding of the importance of effective reflection
- have an overview of the models of reflective practice
- have an appreciation of the methods of clearly articulating experiences through reflection
- have a range of examples exemplifying the different approaches to reflection to compare to your own experience.

Reflection is a part of developing wisdom through experience, enabling you to make wise decisions. This is a very important aspect of being a peer mentor as the decisions you make can affect your mentees quite significantly. Hence careful consideration of what reflection is and how to undertake it effectively is needed.

According to the Collins Dictionary (2006), reflection is defined as 'the act of reflecting, careful or long consideration'. Reflection in this text is addressed as an ongoing process of looking at yourself. As is indicated in the Collins definition, it is a verb and hence not an end in itself. Some of the general characteristics of effective reflection include:

- reviewing your own experience
- analysing your own actions and reactions
- analysing others' actions and reactions
- being willing to learn from experience in light of your reflection.

To aid you in this process we will discuss how you can give careful and long consideration to your own experiences to benefit your development. As you may already know, reflection is utilised in a number of professions to ensure ongoing development and enhancement of practice. These professions have recognised it as an effective tool whereby each individual can examine their own actions, the situations that gave rise to those actions and their own characteristics which influenced their actions. It not only helps them to understand an experience more clearly and know themselves more deeply but also touches upon a wider sphere of understanding. Learning via reflecting on experience is useful for all aspects of our lives, especially those connected with the tricky areas involving connecting with and supporting other people. This interaction with others is a significant part of the role of the peer mentor, making it a rather complex one in need of disentangling to ensure a clear understanding of the experience. This will enable you to effectively articulate this rewarding but often challenging experience and help to develop yourself as a practitioner of peer mentoring. This chapter will guide you through the process of effective reflection and help to ensure you gain the maximum benefit from your peer mentoring experience.

Why reflect? I already know myself

Many people believe they know themselves well. It is only when faced with a range of situations that they realise that they do not know themselves or understand situations quite as well as they thought. This realisation often results in some self-analysis, especially if the situation was a challenging or a significant one. As we will see, self-analysis is an important and sometimes uncomfortable part of reflection.

Activity 9.1

If you cast your mind back over your life to date, did you ever react to a situation in a slightly different way from how you thought you would? Have you wished you said something you didn't, or didn't say something you did? Why do you think this occurred?

Reflection may be thought of as a sort of self and situation brainstorming activity which can be very enlightening if done honestly. Of course, being honest with yourself can be a challenge, and this is part of what learning to reflect effectively is all about. It is only then that meaningful changes can be put in place to enhance practice and aid you in making the best decisions in future.

Truly effective reflection goes deeper than just getting to know yourself. It is a lesson in people: you and others. It involves gaining a deeper appreciation of emotional intelligence, which will help guide you in all interactions throughout your life. As a peer mentor you will experience many different situations and interact with a wide variety of people. Such a variety poses an emotional intelligence learning curve as you strive to understand the implications of differences in culture, background, age, gender and individual circumstances. In your role it is wise to bear in mind that you are there to guide your mentees without the bias or preconceptions which are often associated with such differences. Such biases and preconceptions tend to affect the approach and style of our interactions with other people, although this often happens automatically, involving subtle changes in our communications and interactions. For example, how do you normally engage with particular people in light of their age or ethnicity? Does dealing with someone who is older than you change the way you interact with them? Do you perhaps see them as being out of date with technology, and therefore use an approach and style which might be somewhat patronising? Conversely, you may see them as being wiser than you due to their age and use a style that is less confident than it might be with younger mentees. Being aware of your own preconceptions is an important aspect to include in your reflections, and this should include consideration of your approach and style as this will have a significant impact on the outcome of your mentoring relationships.

As you can see, your approach and style are critical factors for effective mentoring. Approach and style are often included in the reflective activities of a number of professions, especially where success is based around recipients' outcomes or achievements. Such is the case in teaching, counselling and often sports coaching. These professions might be seen as akin to mentoring in that there is no requirement of the participants to listen to or adhere to the advice given. Perhaps unsurprisingly, therefore, many amateur sports coaches strive to inspire when coaching, giving speeches or pep talks to their teams. They realise that in order to get the best out of their players they need to find a way to make them want to and believe they can achieve. The reflection these sports coaches then engage in is in reviewing the effects of their coaching and speeches on the responses from their team. If they feel their team went on to play particularly well or poorly they will reflect on the extent to which this was due to their coaching style or pep talk. They recognise that their approach and style are crucial to motivating their team or athletes. To do this effectively they must know what works for their athletes. It might be that a positively encouraging style of coaching enhances the players' confidence in their training while a supportive approach in their pep talks helps the athletes believe they can win. As a peer mentor you will ideally provide a positively supportive approach to your mentees to help them believe in their own efforts to bring about desired goals. Inspirational leaders tend to have a keen interest in understanding the people who make up their team or group so that they are able to understand what approach and style will work. They develop their emotional intelligence to achieve this through ongoing reflection on self and group analysis. As a peer mentor it will be important to get to know your mentees to enable you to know how to effectively support them.

As a peer mentor you do not have subordinates, you have peers. Essentially, your peers in this situation are more akin to a sports team. Gaining an understanding of not only yourself but also your peers through reflection will produce the best results for all.

Activity 9.2

Consider times when you have been involved with team or group activities. How did your leaders/coaches encourage or persuade you to listen and pay attention to them? Why were some more effective at this than others?

Reflections and perceptions

In the same way that people believe they know themselves, it is also common for people to think they know someone else really well – and equally common to find out they do not. There is a tendency to feel an understanding of someone purely because there has been the development of acquaintance over quite a long period of time or through frequent interactions. However, length of time or frequency of communication does not necessarily equate to understanding the mind or character of another person. It is important to realise how easy and common it is for someone to not be as they seem. Perhaps someone you know is reluctant to show their true self to people, even those they consider to be friends. So it is important to remember that some mentees may feel embarrassed about some aspect of themselves and do everything they can to hide it. They may display certain types of behaviour, perhaps being secretive about where they come from, what they eat, who they see, what they have done prior to coming to university, etc. This is not necessarily intentional on their part as it also depends on the viewer's perception and previous experiences. It may be your or the other mentees' prior experience with issues such as; mental health, drug use, sexuality etc. are influencing this impression. There is, of course, no need or reason for mentees to divulge such personal details, but it may still impact on their behaviour, which is what you as a mentor experience of them. As a mentor you just need to ensure that this experience does not negatively affect how you interact with and support mentees.

Both you and your mentees' perceptions of your interactions and relationship have a significant bearing on the effectiveness of that relationship. Therefore, as a mentor it can be an interesting and useful exercise to ask how other people perceive you. You could begin this by asking your family and close friends: what is their interpretation of your personality, your approach to the relationship with them, their perception of your attitudes to others, etc.? This information can then be used to enhance your understanding of others and perhaps also yourself through honest reflection on the answers and your reaction to them. You may wish to do this exercise with your mentees after you have developed a good relationship with them and there is a good level of trust and communication.

Activity 9.3

Think of a few situations that have occurred in your life where you reacted to the experience in a way that was memorable to you. These might be experiences that stand out in your memory but may not have for other people – for example, your first day at work when you became stressed that you could not take everything in, or when you saw an accident and just froze for a few minutes. These should include personal, professional and educational experiences and one related to your hobby or pastime.

Describe the situation to two or three of your friends or family without telling them what your reaction was and ask them to tell you what they think you would do in these situations. Obviously the situations will have to be ones that they were not involved in, or you could change the details slightly to avoid their connecting with the experience.

How close are your friends or family to describing what your reaction actually was?

Our perceptions of different groups of people are built up over our lives in response to a variety of input, including our own experiences, the perceptions of family members and the media. These perceptions then become preconceptions that we overlay on interactions with other people to bias our thinking. As a mentor you need to guard against this in yourself. Try to put aside such preconceptions and enter interactions with each new mentee with an unbiased mind.

Activity 9.4

Think about the preconceptions you have about different groups of people, such as those from different countries, of a different religion, or of different gender, age or socioeconomic background, etc.

Where did these preconceptions come from?

When to reflect

We all automatically reflect all the time, be it quite fleetingly or as a more in-depth activity. The more structured approach to reflection suggested for mentors requires some consideration of when to conduct this reflection to ensure the most effective and useful outcome. There are some specific points in a peer mentor's journey that might benefit from some specific and targeted reflection, including:

- when applying for the role
- after your peer mentor training
- after your first session/meeting with your mentees
- after your first peer mentor debrief session
- when you are halfway through the peer programme
- at the end of the peer programme/after the final session
- in preparation for and during the final debrief session
- about a month or two after you have finished your role as of peer mentor
- when applying for a job.

Application phase: Reflection here will help you identify how you feel you can meet the requirements of the role.

After training: Reflect on how the training has assisted you to understand the role and how you can use the activities and items addressed in the training to enhance your skills as a mentor. Did the training make you feel more confident or did it make the role seem daunting? Why do you think this?

After the first session: Reflect on what went well and what you were less happy with and why.

After the first debrief: Reflect on the feedback of your fellow mentors and the discussion around this. Is there anything you would like to bring into your sessions and, if so, why?

Halfway: Reflect on your experiences so far. Can you identify whether and how you have changed in any way? How do you propose improving your mentoring skills for the next half?

The end: Reflect back on the whole experience of being a mentor. What have you learnt about yourself? What changes have you made or are you making to yourself? How has your understanding of the role changed?

Final debrief: What do you want to share with your fellow peer mentors? What were the highs and lows of being a peer mentor and what did this teach you about yourself? To what extent can you connect with your fellow peer mentors' experiences?

Looking back: Time can help to process your thoughts and feelings regarding an experience such as being a peer mentor. You are likely to look back over the first few months of the peer programme, but it is important to give this a specific and sufficient time slot in your life to concentrate on reflecting on the whole experience.

Job application: Being a peer mentor can provide a wealth of examples and evidence to support your job application. Most employers are looking for new staff with good transferable skills. This can mean people who will fit into their current team, be able to show initiative, have good organisational and time management skills, etc. Your role as a peer mentor will have helped you enhance all of these skills. You will need to reflect on your experience and identify examples of where and how you can demonstrate these skills.

Effective reflection requires a structured approach to ensure the best gains from the process. Identifying suitable points for reflection is a key aspect of this and should be considered from the outset. The above time points are suggestions to aid in this, but you may find that there are other moments where some targeted reflection would be helpful.

Models and methods of reflection

Reflection is a learning process: it helps us to understand the reasons for the outcomes of a situation and to learn from that experience. Schon (1991) put forward the idea that reflection could be in-action or on-action. Reflection in-action is where reflection occurs quickly while you are undertaking the experience. On the other hand, reflection on-action might be a much slower process, looking back at an experience at some point after the experience has ended. Reflection on-action permits a slower, more systematic approach which tends to encompass consideration of all factors, including how you reflected in-action. This lends itself to personal development and an opportunity for effective skill development, as well as clearer future planning. Hence reflection in-action and on-action are intertwined activities which feed into each other. As you reflect on your own experiences as a mentor, try to notice how your thoughts and feelings both connect and change between your in-action and your on-action reflection. Often, as you look back on an experience, you identify aspects of your in-action reflection that were not helpful, and this can result in a learning process.

Each of your experiences therefore provides a learning opportunity through reflection, enabling you to become more competent in that situation. This learning space is embodied in the ongoing cyclical reflective process. It is a constant activity that we all undertake automatically throughout our lives. When applying it to being a mentor it takes on a more structured approach, using models to guide the process.

A number of models and methods assist in reflective practice. Common reflective processes involve considering an experience, what happened and how you reacted to it, what the result of that reaction was, and what you would do next time in the same or, similar situation. Various factors can contribute to the effectiveness of your reflection, such as trying to look at the situation from different stakeholders' perspectives as suggested by Brookfield's (1995) Four Lenses. This approach translates as looking at an experience from your own perspective as well as that of your mentees, your fellow mentors and your peer programme organiser. This obviously incorporates input from others as well as your own self-analysis, which provides a richer base for your reflection. One avenue for gaining input from others is to employ a peer observation process, which generally involves mentors observing each others' sessions and making notes on their style,

Diagram representing Brookfield's Four Lenses

communication, content, etc. Not only will you gain input on your sessions, but also you will learn from observing your fellow mentors' sessions. The result of this is a rich source of comment on the session for both participants. It permits discussion that helps clarify the points made and consider alternatives. This joint reflection activity offers avenues to consider new approaches and possible adjustments to your planning activities which can be incorporated into your reflection. Peer observation is utilised in a number of professions to inform and support the development of practice. As a practitioner of peer mentoring you will no doubt find this a useful and supportive activity that will aid you in developing and enhancing your practice.

Another common strategy for reflection is to use the significant incident approach, which considers your views, assumptions, perspectives, interpretations and possible alternative actions. In combining these approaches you may see that you will incorporate a number of perspectives and angles providing a 360 degree review of a situation or experience.

The cycle of reflective learning diagram provides a pictorial representation of the process of learning from experience. This involves reflection on your actions and reactions, and those of the others involved. Further to this is a consideration of their feedback and your reaction to that. At this point you may have some initial thoughts or decisions about what you should have done and what you might

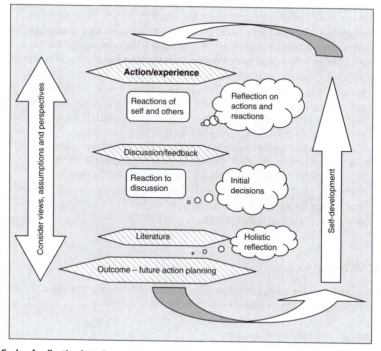

Cycle of reflective learning

do in a future similar situation. Reference to appropriate literature will add to your consideration of the experience and help you make sense of the situation. All aspects can then be brought into your reflection to provide a holistic approach to this process. The whole process is influenced by your views, assumptions and perspectives, which need to be borne in mind throughout your reflection. The outcome is your planning and decisions for future situations which will be achieved through your own self-development and learning.

Activity 9.5

Think of an experience you have had that involved others, where you acted or reacted in a way that you were not completely satisfied with.

Try reflecting on this using the Four Lenses approach. What changes might you wish to make to your actions or reactions?

Case study 9.1: Group reflection using four lenses approach in PAL

PAL mentors are encouraged to reflect on and feed back to the peer programme organiser to aid development and enhancement of the scheme. This generally occurs at the end of the term when all mentors are brought together to exchange and discuss experiences, challenges, successes, etc. The mentors reflected on the sessions they had led and noted that these sometimes became unfocused as mentees did not know how to identify what they needed to address. This reflection and discussion resulted in suggestions from mentors that there needed to be more structure to the sessions. They felt that the flexibility in the topics of the sessions was well intentioned but gave the impression of a lack of organisation and direction. They noted that this made them feel uncomfortable and not able to effectively fulfil their role. It was also noted that they felt that this did not support mentees in the best manner and tended to cause disengagement. The literature, which indicated that structure is a key ingredient in the success of a programme, supported this view. As a result it was agreed that the scheme would adopt a more structured style, which proved to be appreciated by the mentees.

How to reflect

The models provide a foundation for your reflection. As you start to reflect, bear in mind the aspects noted in these models, including:

- your preconceptions and assumptions
- your expectations

- your interpretation of others' perceptions and expectations
- your reaction to the experience
- your reaction to others' reactions and feedback.

In undertaking your reflection, try to really consider your inner thoughts and feelings about the experience and all aspects relating to this. You may wish to analyse your experience by asking yourself some questions. These will relate to your actions and feelings, including:

- What did I do and why?
- What did I feel and why?
- What was my reaction and why?
- What were others' reactions and why do I think they reacted in that way?

Looking back at an experience gives you the opportunity to connect some of your assumptions and preconceptions to your actions, reactions and interpretations. Analysing your experiences in this way is not a quick process. It takes time to really think about an experience, and honestly pull out your assumptions and draw on your inner preconceptions. Experimenting in your mind to find possible connections between these areas can be a very challenging exercise. As human beings we are somewhat shy of being really honest with ourselves and the reflective process will help you overcome this tricky area.

First, we need to accept that we make mistakes and this is normal and acceptable. We also need to recognise that others make mistakes too, which is equally normal and acceptable. Unfortunately our society tends to want to find someone to blame for anything that does not go completely right, causing us to feel that making mistakes is somehow a failing. This tends to lead to people not being really honest with themselves, for fear of feeling a failure. However, your own reflection is a good and safe place to really start recognising your own tendencies to blame others, or situations, etc. Part of this recognition connects with your emotional reactions in terms of how an experience made you feel? Were you sad, upset, hurt, joyful, satisfied, contented, etc.? What actually triggered these feelings? If you've come out of a peer session feeling less than happy and perhaps wondering if you should bother continuing, are you able to identify what triggered this reaction in you? Did you feel your mentees were not interested in what you had to say, did not agree with you, seemed to think the session was a waste of time, made you feel less than adequate, made you feel unwanted and unappreciated, etc.? Finding connections between the experience of being a peer mentor and your connected emotional reactions is a key aspect of the reflective process. Once you have started to be able to find these connections in yourself, you can then consider the reactions of others and their possible emotional basis.

In attempting to undertake this testing task it can be useful to write your thoughts down. The very process of writing things down can help you to really grapple with your own thoughts as you have to formulate your emotions, perceptions and interpretations into something. However, this does not have to be just text; you could use a mind map, or other pictorial approach, which would help you to examine your thoughts. This could then be used to connect with your records of your experience as a peer mentor.

Recording your experiences

To maximise the potential of reflection you will need to find a way to record your experiences that suits you. Flanagan (1954) proposed a critical incident technique to aid in observing and understanding the reasons for the actions of people in different situations. This approach has been widely adopted, with many adaptations to suit the particular industry or field of study.

A quite commonly applied significant incident approach to reflection and analysis involves considering:

- Why did you view the situation as you did?
- What assumptions did you have about the people, situation or place?
- What other interpretations could you have made?
- What alternative actions could you have taken?
- How will you deal with a similar situation in future?
- With hindsight, how do you wish you had dealt with the situation?
- With hindsight, do you think you could have done something differently given your knowledge and skills at that point?

Recording your experiences in this way takes practice to ensure you get the most out of the exercise. Keep records as you go; do not wait until the end of term. This will ensure that you capture the nuances of your thoughts which you can further reflect on later with hindsight – your on-action reflection. Try to record the thoughts that you had during the activity – capturing your in-action reflection. The process of reflection takes time and concentration, so find a location that you find comfortable and conducive to thinking about your experiences. You may find it useful to have a reflection routine to aid you in this activity. Perhaps start by making a few quick notes immediately after the experience, including the date, place, people involved and a brief description of what happened. Turning the above list into a table might be a useful tool to prompt you to consider the different angles (see the example table on page 103).

When considering writing about one of your experiences in a significant incident style, you first need to decide what constitutes an experience worthy of your consideration. The way to decide this is to think about all your experiences and consider what you feel you gained out of the different situations. Did you learn something about yourself, about how other people tend to react or perhaps about how groups interact? It might be that a situation posed a conundrum for you that you struggled to contend with, which would benefit from deeper consideration.

Once you have identified your suitable experiences you can use the significant incident table to work through the various aspects of reflection.

Significant Incident Table of Reflection

Experience:	(Briefly describe experience)	Date:
Persons involved:		
Aspect	Immediate thoughts	Further reflection
Why did you view the situation as you did?		
What assumptions did you have about the people, situation or place?		
What other interpretations could you have made?		
What alternative actions could you have taken?		
How will you deal with a similar situation in future?		
With hindsight, how do you wish you had dealt with the situation?		
With hindsight, do you think you could have done something differently given your knowledge and skills at that point?		

It can be a good idea to quickly note your immediate thoughts on an experience. This will give you your 'gut reaction' to that experience. These thoughts might be quite emotional and be influenced by your preconceptions, attitudes and current state of mind. The thoughts you have about an experience can be significantly affected by your emotional state, hence if you are feeling frustrated, annoyed or another negative emotion your views of an experience will be coloured by this. As you undertake your further reflection you can incorporate your thoughts about how this emotional state affected your actions and reactions.

Activity 9.6

Try reflecting on one of your experiences using the critical incident approach.

Case study: The critical incident approach

A mentee reported feeling very homesick and unable to cope with university life. They were considering giving up doing their degree and leaving the university to return home.

The mentor listened to the mentee's concerns and asked them some questions about whether they enjoyed their chosen subject, to which the mentee affirmed their interest. The mentor noted that it is normal to feel homesick in the first few weeks at university and that this would pass. The mentor suggested that the mentee speak to their personal tutor and join some students' union groups.

The mentee did not speak to their personal tutor or join any students' union groups. They stayed with the programme until the Christmas break but then did not return after the break. The mentor felt disappointed and almost annoyed with the mentee for not doing what they had advised.

When reflecting on this experience the mentor realised that they had assumed the mentee would be comfortable approaching the personal tutor to discuss their concerns. They had also assumed that the mentee would be comfortable joining students' union groups as they themselves had done. When reflecting on this from an emotional intelligence point of view they realised that they did not really know the mentee. They did not find out whether they would be reluctant to speak to the personal tutor or join students' union groups. As they had not gained an understanding of the perceptions and views of the mentee, they realised that the advice given may not have been the best avenue to take. In reviewing the literature they also gained an appreciation of the variation in reactions of different people. This was affirmed through discussion with other mentors and support staff.

The mentor reflected on possible interpretations of the actions or inactions of the mentee. Perhaps they were not comfortable in approaching their personal tutor due to differences in gender, age and cultural background. Also, possibly prior experience with (demographically) similar persons might have influenced how the mentee felt about the situation and advice given.

The mentor also reflected on why they themselves reacted with disappointment and annoyance towards the mentee. In considering this more deeply they realised that they were frustrated that the mentee had not told them they were not comfortable approaching their personal tutor, but that this in itself would have been difficult for the mentee to say. Further reflection on this situation brought the mentor to an understanding of the importance of getting to know their mentees.

The mentor decided to ensure that there were more opportunities to learn about their mentees early on in the term. They also suggested asking personal tutors and support staff to attend a group peer meeting to ensure that mentees met these staff in a comfortable environment.

Relating experiences to development

How one applies the new thinking resulting from reflection is of course the key aspect to enhancement. There is no point in having a significant revelation or 'light bulb' moment if you do nothing with it.

In considering what we can learn from reflection it is important to think about where you have come from and also perhaps what you want your endpoint to be. With respect to self-development you can then begin to make a plan to get you there. This process will use the information and understanding you gained through your honest reflection. Your plan might then include starting with reviewing where you were when you started the reflection activities. Looking back with hindsight, can you now identify which areas you are happy with and what you feel would benefit from changes? When undertaking this step you can also consider why you are happy with some aspects but not others. This should also connect with your desired endpoint. What type of person will you be and what will your perceptions, attitudes, confidence, organisation and approach be as this more self-aware person?

For the areas where you identify a need for change, consider the following:

- Can you pinpoint exactly what it is that you would like to change?
- Have you recognised a trend in your own actions and reactions over time?
- Have you gradually become more organised or confident?
- From reviewing your reflection notes, do you feel a change might result in a more useful and agreeable outcome in future?

Perhaps you recognise that you have a tendency to become defensive, annoyed or upset in certain types of situation, which influences how you react to such situations. It might be that as a peer mentor you became defensive when a mentee questioned the information or advice you were giving. This led to you giving a response that to your mentees made you seem annoyed, resulting in a less than productive session. The outcome might have been that the session upset you, making you feel uncomfortable and injuring your confidence. In reflecting on this you might note that the main issue for you was your reaction to a mentee questioning your knowledge. Hence what you might decide to try to change is your tendency to react defensively. Just being aware of your own inclinations is a significant step towards self-development.

Making such changes is not easy. It takes time, considerable effort and above all a true desire to change. You need to bear in mind here that this is only about making changes to yourself. You cannot and should not attempt to change someone else, although as a peer mentor you might suggest that your mentees try this reflective exercise for themselves. This could be supported with some group reflection to assist your mentees to really understand the process clearly.

Activity 9.7

Consider to what extent you are comfortable making changes to yourself. Reflect on your reasoning and try to identify your barriers to change.

How good was that?

Reflecting on your actions, successes, disappointments and perhaps failures can be a hugely rewarding and enlightening experience. Developing your skills in this area will help you throughout your life in all activities and relationships you might experience. Being a peer mentor provides an ideal training ground to hone these skills in a supported environment.

Looking back on your experiences, not only as a peer mentor but also over the rest of your life in an actively engaged, reflective manner, will offer the optimal avenue for self-development. Ongoing on- and in-action reflection will also help to ensure that you are an effective mentor for the duration of your role in your peer programme. Being effective in any role makes it a rewarding activity in and of itself. You will be able to look back on your experiences as a mentor in the future and feel that you achieved something useful. It is likely that your own development will be key. This book is designed to help you make the most out of your peer mentor experience and ensure that it is a good one both for your mentees and, perhaps more importantly, for yourself.

Conclusion

This chapter has introduced you to the concept, methods and theories of reflection. It has explained the importance of reflection for your own development, both as a mentor and for your future career and life activities. The ability to reflect honestly and with a 360 degree view is a key skill used by many professions to ensure service quality and staff self-actualisation. Effective methods of reflection to ensure this whole-picture approach include Brookfield's Four Lenses and the critical incident technique. As a mentor it is important to find a method that suits you and that will enable you to effectively articulate your reflection on your experiences. This in turn will support and guide your self-development, enabling a greater understanding of emotional intelligence for all your future experiences.

It is through this candid reflection that you will be able to appreciate the suggestion that reflection is paramount to personal development and offers a process enabling you to learn from your experiences.

Key points from this chapter

- Be aware of your thoughts and emotional standpoint during an experience.
- Quickly note down your immediate thoughts and feelings in response to an experience.
- Include thoughts and responses from others in your reflection.
- Identify areas for self-development based on your honest reflection.

Conclusion

In writing this book we have provided an overview of peer-led learning in higher education. We have looked at what mentoring at university in the 21st century is and the opportunities and challenges it presents. You have been introduced to the role and place of peer mentoring in universities. Mentors play a vital part in various aspects of universities' strategies, such as helping to address retention, promoting achievement, supporting student diversity and equality, and assisting with transition into and within higher education. Mentors also help universities in less formal ways, such as by enabling enhanced interaction with peers, providing opportunities for students to become more engaged with their courses, and being an additional mechanism for feedback and communication between staff and students.

Various mentoring models are used by universities, from quite structured approaches such as peer-assisted learning (PAL) and peer-assisted study sessions (PASS) to more informal arrangements. Mentoring practice at university is developing at a rapid rate, with new practices and innovations all the time. These are happening in all sorts of areas, but most notably there are current innovations in online mentoring, mentoring to support diversity, mentoring at postgraduate level, and mentoring leadership for experienced mentors to further develop their skills and help to support new mentors. Regardless of the model adopted, all stakeholders can benefit from the experience, including you as a peer mentor. The extent to which you benefit from this experience depends largely on what you put into it.

Throughout the book you have been introduced to some of the ideas which underpin peer mentoring at university. First, learning is 'socially constructed', that is, it takes place in a social context, through discussion and meaning making, whereby a learner takes on new information by fitting it into what they already know. Second, mentoring is 'situated learning', which means that new information must be situated in an authentic or relevant context. This involves applying learning to real situations or experiences. As a mentor you will be able to help your mentees to apply their newly acquired knowledge to authentic situations which will help them to understand and process the information they encounter in books and lectures. Third, mentors play an important part in student transition, helping newer students to move from peripheral participation in university life to being engaged and integrated members of a learning community (Wenger, 1989). Finally, mentoring activity has various labels such as 'facilitating' or 'scaffolding' (Brown, Collins and Duguid, 1989). Nevertheless, the focus here is on the mentor providing a framework which enables their mentee(s) to learn through their own endeavour and experience rather than doing things for them.

Evaluating mentoring

There is now a strong emphasis on evaluating the impact of mentoring schemes. Your university will already have its own ways to monitor and evaluate mentoring. However, you may find it useful and interesting to evaluate yourself as a mentor. This can be done in many different ways. Below are some things to consider.

What type of evidence might be useful?

When you evaluate something you first need to decide what your aim was so that you can measure outcomes against this. For example, some mentoring programmes aim to give students support with specific skills such as maths or academic writing. Other schemes aim to support students' transition into university. Others aim to improve student engagement. The evidence that you gather will depend on what your own aim was. Therefore if your aim is to improve students' maths skills, you might decide to set a maths test before and after mentoring intervention. If your aim is to help students settle in to university, you may use a questionnaire (for example an online survey tool) to find out students' feelings towards the university before and after mentoring, etc.

How can data be collected?

Data can be collected through formal means such as questionnaires, interviews or focus groups, or it can be gathered through documents such as assignment grades or attendance registers.

Designing a questionnaire or interview

Mentors can do their own research into mentoring. If you want to design your own survey or questionnaire there are some things to remember. First, decide whether you will use closed or open questions. Closed questions do not allow for any variety of answer but can be useful to observe trends. Open questions allow for variety, but this means that answers are hard to collate or compare. Questions can be asked online via a survey, written on paper or asked face to face. There are pros and cons to all of these formats. An online questionnaire is tidy and can be anonymous, but often people ignore them. A paper survey can be handed out to mentees in a group or individually. There is more chance that they will answer it but less anonymity. A focus group of interviewees allows you to ask follow-up questions and have a dialogue with your mentees, but they may not answer entirely truthfully and it is not anonymous. The answers you get will be varied so it may be impossible to draw conclusions. Remember to keep in mind always what it is you want to find out. This should help you decide how you will design your questionnaire.

Presenting your findings

Usually at the end of an academic year you will be given a chance to give your own feedback on mentoring. If you have been doing your own evaluation, this will be greatly valued by mentoring support staff. You may get a chance to make a short presentation or give verbal feedback, or you may be asked to write a report. If you have generated data through a survey or document analysis it is very useful to present this. You can do this visually using graphs, which often have greater impact than descriptive writing. There may even be an opportunity for you to present some of your findings at the annual national peer-led learning conference. When you are presenting your findings, always think about your audience and what it is they need to know. This way your information can be relevant and targeted.

Activity 10.1

Design your own questionnaire to evaluate your mentoring, using the template below if you wish.

Questions to consider	Responses
What is your aim as a mentor?	
Are you planning to ask online or face-to-face questions?	
Do you intend to gather the demographic details of respondents? If so, what do you want to know? • age • gender • ethnicity • entry qualification • first language, etc.	
What questions will you ask? • Will you use a Likert scale for respondents to rate answers or not? • Will you have any closed questions? • Will you have any open questions? • Will you allow more than one answer?	
How will you present your findings?	
Who will you present your findings to?	

Innovations and improvements to any project are usually based on evidence, so if what you present provides evidence for a change to the way in which mentoring is done, your research will in a small way have contributed to that development.

Final word

Peer-led learning has the potential to transform the way in which learning takes place. This book has focused on the role of peer mentors at universities and how to improve and develop what you do. Mentoring is overwhelmingly a good experience, and if you carry out your role well you can have a positive impact on your mentees' development. It is also a relatively new role which is still very much evolving, thus it is an exciting and dynamic area to work in. This means that mentors' input is highly regarded and therefore your suggestions and feedback on how to develop the role are likely to be valued. We wish you well in your role as peer mentors.

Appendix

Peer mentor characteristics review table

Consider the following and rate to what extent you agree with each item.

Item: I am ...	Completely agree (5)	Moderately agree (4)	Neutral (3)	Disagree (2)	Completely disagree (1)
A. an outgoing person					
B. considered to be reliable					
B. neat and organised					
A. productive and task oriented					
B. compassionate					
B. able to talk to anyone					
B. full of ideas					
B. lacking in patience					
B. never late					
B. a keen participant in individual sports and activities					
B. thought to be considerate					
B. a list maker					
B. highly motivated					
C. honest and direct with others					
C. often behind with work and tasks					
C. happier on my own					
B. persistent					
A. good at team games and activities					

Item: I am ...	Completely agree (5)	Moderately agree (4)	Neutral (3)	Disagree (2)	Completely disagree (1)
C. wary of others' intentions					
C. a person who likes to lead and direct					
B. creative					
A. generally very happy					
C. not interested in others' goals					
A. told I'm a good listener					
A. eager to share					
A. always courteous					
B. inquisitive					
C. comfortable arguing my point					
C. upset when things go wrong and I feel like giving up					
B. loyal to my friends and colleagues					
A. sensitive to others' feelings					

Generally speaking the A items relate to interpersonal aspects, the B items relate to intrapersonal characteristics and the C items relate to conflict/agreeableness tendencies.

You should note that this is not a test or evaluation of your personality; it is a reflection activity to aid you in thinking about yourself and how you deal with situations and people. Your responses may well be quite varied or may be quite similar for each characteristic. Your responses are neither a negative nor a positive reflection on you, they just indicate a possible bias or an even array of characteristics. This is something for you to reflect on and decide whether you wish to try to enhance any particular aspect.

To connect your responses to Terrion and Leonard's characteristics you might regard interpersonal aspects as correlating with communication, interdependent attitude and personality match. These are characteristics where you connect well with your mentees through good communication, sharing experiences and being open-minded.

Intrapersonal aspects refer to your inner personal characteristics, including empathy, supportiveness and self-motivation. This is where having a deep appreciation of others' situations and feelings is displayed, as well as your inner drive.

The last area of conflict and agreeableness refers to your tendency to want to take charge and be task oriented. These are not necessarily negative attributes as groups often benefit from some clear direction, as long as there is good support and flexibility from the mentor.

The usefulness of undertaking this exercise is in the reflection that you do on yourself. What do your responses tell you about yourself?

References

Ashman, M. and Colvin, J. (2010) Roles, risks, and benefits of peer mentoring relationships in higher education. *Mentoring & Tutoring: Partnerships in Learning*, 18(2), 121–134.

Bloom, B.S., Engelhart, M.D., Furst, E.J., Hill, W.H. and Krathwohl, D.R. (1956) *Taxonomy of Educational Objectives: The Classification of Educational Goals. Handbook I: Cognitive Domain*. New York: David McKay Company.

Brookfield, S. (1995) *Becoming a Critically Reflective Teacher*. San Francisco: Jossey-Bass.

Brown, J.S., Collins, A. and Duguid, P. (1989) Situated cognition and the culture of learning. *American Educator*, 18(1), 32–42.

Brown, K., Nairn, K., van der Meer, J. and Scott, C. (2014) 'We were told we're not teachers ... It gets difficult to draw the line': Negotiating roles in peer-assisted study sessions (PASS). *Mentoring & Tutoring: Partnership in Learning*, 22(2), 146–161.

Buzan, T. (2002) *How to Mind Map*. London: Harper Collins.

Collins Paperback Dictionary, (5th ed.) (2006) Glasgow: Harper Collins Publishers.

Connor, K.M. and Davidson, J.R.T. (2003) Development of a new resilience scale: The Connor and Davidson resilience scale (CD-RISC). *Depress Anxiety*, 18(2), 76–82.

Donelan, M. (1999) SI Leaders: The Real Winners. Kansas City: National Conference on Supplemental Instruction., 20–22 May.

Dosad, J. (2015) Graphic recording. Available at: http://www.banter.uk.net/ [accessed 10 October 2016].

Eldridge, D. and Wilson, E. (2003) Nurturing knowledge: The UK Higher Education Links Scheme. *Public Administration & Development*, 23(2), 151–164.

Equality and Human Rights Commission, Equality Act (2010) Creating a Fairer Britain. Available at: http://www.equalityhumanrights.com/legal-and-policy/legislation/equality-act-2010 [accessed 14 January 2016].

Flanagan, J.C. (1954) The critical incident technique. *Psychological Bulletin*, 51(4), 327–58.

Frey, D.L. and Gaertner, S.L. (1986) Helping and the avoidance of inappropriate interracial behavior: A strategy that perpetuates a non-prejudiced self-image. *Journal of Personality and Social Psychology*, 50(6), 1083–1090.

Gibbs, G. (1988) *Learning by Doing: A Guide to Teaching and Learning Methods*. London: Further Education Unit.

Goleman, D. (1995) *Emotional Intelligence*. New York: Bantam Books.

Goleman, D. (1996) *Emotional Intelligence: Why It Can Matter More than IQ*. London: Bloomsbury Publishing.

Goleman, D. (1998) What makes a leader. *Harvard Business Review*, Nov/Dec(6), 93–102.

Goleman, D. (2001) *The Emotionally Intelligent Workplace*. San Francisco: Jossey-Bass.

Green, P. (2011) A literature review of peer-assisted learning: National HE STEM programme's project: 'Peer-assisted learning: In and beyond the classroom'. Available at: http://www.hestem-sw.org.uk/project?id=13&pp=78 [accessed 23 September 2016].

Hammond, J., Bithell, C., Jones, L. and Bidwood, P. (2010) A first year experience of student-directed peer-assisted learning. *Active Learning in Higher Education*, (11), 201–212.

Johnston, D. and Johnston, R. (1991) *Active Learning: Cooperation in the College Classroom.* Minesota: Interaction Book Company.

Keenan, C. (2014) Mapping student-led learning in the UK. Available at: https://www.heacademy.ac.uk/sites/default/files/resources/peer_led_learning_keenan_nov_14-final.pdf [accessed 22 September 2015].

Keenan, C. and Benjamin, L. (2012) Making PALS! A meta-evaluation of adopters' activities. Available at http://www.hestem-sw.org.uk/project?id=13&pp=527 [accessed 5 July 2015].

Kelly, J. (2002) Collaborative learning: Higher education, interdependence, and the authority of knowledgy by Kenneth Bruffee: A critical study. *Journal of the National Collegiate Honors Council – Online Archive*, Spring/Summer, 90–100.

Klasen N & Clutterbuck. D (2001) *Implementing Mentoring Schemes* Butterworth-Heinemann.

Kolb, D.A. (1984) *Experiential Learning.* Englewood Cliffs, NJ: Prentice Hall.

Mayer, J.D. and Salovey, P. (1993) The intelligence of emotional intelligence. *Intelligence*, 17(4), 433–442.

Mayer, J.D. and Salovey, P. (1997) What is emotional intelligence? In: P. Salovey and D. Sluyter (eds) *Emotional Development and Emotional Intelligence: Implications for Educators.* New York: Basic Books, pp. 3–31.

Micari, M., Streitwieser, B. and Light, G. (2005) Undergraduates leading undergraduates: Peer facilitation in a science workshop program. *Innovative Higher Education*, 30(4), 269–288.

MIND (2013) Available at: http://www.mind.org.uk/information-support/a-z-mental-health/ [accessed 5 October 2016].

Myers-Briggs, I. (2011) MBTI today. Available at: http://mbtitoday.org/ [accessed 5 October 2016].

NHS. Available at: http://www.nhs.uk/Livewell/mentalhealth/Pages/Mentalhealthhome.aspx [accessed 5 October 2016].

Norris, D., Lefrere, P. and Mason, J. (2006) Making knowledge services work in higher education. *Educause Review*, Sept/Oct, 84–93.

Ody, M. and Carey, W. (2013) Peer education. In: E. Dunne and D. Owen (eds) *The Student Engagement Handbook: Practice in Higher Education.* Bingley: Emerald Group Publishing, pp. 291–312.

Rogers, C. (1951) *Client-Centered Therapy: Its Current Practice, Implications and Theory.* London: Constable.

Schon, D. (1984) *The Reflective Practitioner: How Professionals Think in Action.* New York: Basic Books.

Schon, D. (1991) *The Reflective Practitioner: How Professionals Think in Action.* Aldershot: Ashgate Publishing.

Schroeder, D., Penner, L., Dovidio, J. and Piliavin, J. (1998) *The Psychology of Helping and Altruism.* New York: McGraw-Hill.

Skalicky, J. and Caney, A. (2010) PASS student leader and mentor roles: A tertiary leadership pathway. *Journal of Peer Learning*, 3(1), 24–37.

Smathers, A.G. (2003) *Guide to the Isabel Briggs Myers Papers 1885–1992.* University of Florida Libraries, Department of Special and Area Studies Collections, Gainesville, FL. Retrieved 5 December 2005.

Terrion, J.L. and Leonard, D. (2007) A taxonomy of the characteristics of student peer mentors in higher education: Findings from a literature review. *Mentoring &Tutoring: Partnership in Learning,* 15(2), 149–164.

University of Kent (2016) Careers and employability service. Available at: https://www.kent.ac.uk/careers/sk/top-ten-skills.htm [acccessed 3 July 2016].

Vygotsky, L.S. (1978). Interaction between learning and development. In: *Mind in Society: The Development of Higher Psychological Processes.* Cambridge, MA: Harvard University Press, pp. 79–91.

Wenger, E. (1998) *Communities of Practice: Learning, Meaning and Identity.* New York: Cambridge University Press.

Zacharopoulou, A., Giles, M. and Condell, J. (2015) Enhancing PASS leaders' employability skills through reflection. *Journal of Learning Development in Higher Education. Special Edition: Academic Peer Learning,* November, 1–19.

Index